Cricket On
Three Continents

Cricket On
Three Continents

Henry Blofeld

WP
WYMER
PUBLISHING
Bedford, England

First published in 1970
This edition published 2015 by Wymer Publishing
Bedford, England
www.wymerpublishing.co.uk
Tel: 01234 326691
Wymer Publishing is a trading name of Wymer (UK) Ltd

ISBN 978-1-908724-34-2

Background image courtesy of Dr. Drew Thompson
Henry Blofeld portrait © Emma Brünjes Productions.

Printed and bound by
Clays, Suffolk, England

A catalogue record for this book is available from the British Library.

Cover design by Andy Bishop.

Contents

FOREWORD

In the eighteen months before this book was written, three major cricket tours took place involving the West Indies, England and Australia. One was held in each country, West Indies v England, Australia v West Indies and England v West Indies and this period saw the final collapse of the famous West Indies side of the early and middle 1960's.

Cricket and the West Indies are therefore two threads going through the book and I make the third. On a cricket tour, and this was the reason for my going to the West Indies and Australia, it is easy to spend most of one's life with the group of people with whom one is travelling and to see a limited amount of the countries and their people.

In both countries I did what I could to see something of both and I had some amusing and interesting adventures which were in a sense a long way removed from cricket, but which helped to give me more of an insight into the cricket of each country as well as the country itself. They were adventures I had largely on my own and by oneself one is better able to see a country unselfconsciously as it is.

In each of these countries, although the rules are the same, cricket becomes almost a different game. In a strange way the mood of the country seems to dictate the tempo at which it is played as well as the approach of its own national side. In these pages I have followed my own experiences in the West Indies and Australia to try to bring to life the atmosphere of these two countries and the characteristics of their people.

I have written about one Test Match in each trying to show how the atmosphere and character of a country is found on the cricket field. Only two Test Matches are written about in full for this is not intended to be a catalogue of ageing figures, but an attempt to look at the human element in cricket on the field by looking at the countries which produce the players and using the cricket to illustrate and develop my theme.

Most people will remember the West Indies v England series for the riot Test at Kingston or for Sobers' declaration which gave England the match at Port of Spain or the final Test at Georgetown when Jones played out the last agonising over from Gibbs to save the series for England. I have, however, taken the First Test which produced some of the best cricket of the whole series and was a match to satisfy the sensationalist and the romantic as well as the aesthete. In Australia I have written about the only drawn match of the five which was also by a long way the most exciting, a curious paradox of cricket.

For the rest I have taken my own experiences in these two countries and have based my impressions on them . . . It is a personal book, a book about cricket although cricket is only part of the book.

I

The problems ahead

It was eight o'clock in the evening and it was hot. The warm air tinged with the smell of oil and grease, felt momentarily unreal, like the first few seconds in a Turkish bath. There were shadowy figures walking towards the aeroplane in the dark and a great many heads looked through the windows of the airport building. Then suddenly the Low Tenor, the Double Second, the High Tenor, the Guitar Pan, the High Cello, the Cello Bass and the Bass among several others, came in on the first note together. The wind blew the noise out to the runway, other figures came running and flash bulbs blinked.

The 1967/68 MCC tour of the West Indies had started amid the excitement, the enthusiasm and the unexpected which were to form its constant backcloth for the next three and a half months. Photographs, interviews, handshakes, more photographs, then the band changed to 'Island In The Sun' and more people surged forward to get their first glimpse of Colin Cowdrey and his men. The steel band were playing by the entrance to the airport building, keeping up a fast rhythm as the MCC party, fifteen hours away from a drizzling London, carried their hand luggage wearily into the Customs Hall.

After the bags had been marked and a drink in the VIP lounge, the big crowd in the car park at the back got their first glimpse of Colin Milburn of whom they had heard so much. They were amazed at his size and with Milburn grinning they asked him how he was going to deal with "big Wes and Charlie". Milburn put down his bag and played an imaginary hook and they roared with delight. When he was in the car those near enough put their hands through the window to shake his, and those further away shouted and waved until the car was out of sight. They had waited a long time, since 1959/60, for this tour. They had eagerly anticipated it and they were going to enjoy every moment.

Slowly the cars eased their way out of the airport leaving the crowd to discuss what they had seen, and conversation, no doubt, went on a long time.

The first few moments of a tour are the exciting climax of weeks of preparation. But they are anxious times too. The captain and the fifteen men around him were on their own. The selectors had met and talked and selected. For four months it had been easy and maybe comforting to sit at home in front of a fire and to say that England had a very good chance, that Hall and Griffith were past it, and that Sobers was the only man to fear and there was a limit to what he could do on his own. Each player had been picked to do a job and now at last it was up to him to do it. In a sense, when the aeroplane landed, each man was on his own. Several of the party had not played in the West Indies before and they would not have been human if amongst the general excitement they had not felt some slight apprehension. The more experienced players had reputations to guard and they may also have been wondering just how things were going to work out. Each one of the party must have been only too well aware that every tour throws up its failures as well as its successes.

There could have been no one more aware of the implications of success and failure than Cowdrey as he made his first speech of the tour and looked forward to an exciting series of attractive cricket. Cowdrey had played more Test cricket than anyone in the party and he had been on more tours. He knew the individual and the collective snags. His own form at home in recent seasons had made him rather less than an automatic choice for England. He had seen touring sides flounder for lack of discipline; on each of his tours he had seen players washed up as failures and he had noticed the effect it had had on them. But this was the first tour that had been his although he had been given the captaincy in unenviable circumstances. One captain, Close, had been dispossessed, another, Smith, had announced his retirement as soon as Close had been dropped and so once again the selectors had fallen back on Cowdrey whom they had sacked from the captaincy a year before. They now made it plain that his appointment was not their first choice.

There were people who said that Close should never have

been dropped. There were others saying that England was bound to lose with Cowdrey as captain, and there was almost no one who had not pre-judged either the captain or the tour. Cowdrey's own future was therefore heavily bound up with the progress of England in the West Indies. The most convincing answer was for him to take the Wisden trophy back to Lord's at the beginning of April.

Leaving the captaincy apart, MCC left Heathrow on December 27th seemingly with nothing more than an outside chance of taking on the West Indies, the "World Champions", in their own climate, and beating them. Since the 1960/61 tour of Australia when Worrell's side tied the First Test although they went on to lose that series, the West Indies had been unbeaten. They changed captains in the middle of this period, Sobers taking over from Worrell, but they went on winning. Theirs was a great side. Their strength came from a combination of the pace of Hall and Griffith, the exciting strokeplay of Sobers, Kanhai and Nurse and the off-spin of Gibbs as well as the ability of Sobers to bowl three different ways and to take unbelievable catches at short-leg.

For more than six years the West Indies had swept all before them as a great side should, but now anno domini was beginning to have an effect. Conrad Hunte, who through the years had been about the most consistent if not the most eye-catching of their batsmen, had retired; the fierce pace of Hall and Griffith had been blunted and the whole side was looking that much more fallible. It may seem rather desperate when a side bases its best chance of success, as England did now, on such vague hopes, but it was perfectly reasonable. The West Indies had played the same side for so long that when at last it began to break up they did not have the players with the experience to come into the side and take over. A great deal too was going to depend on Sobers, the outstanding cricketer of the generation, who was four cricketers in one and, at thirty-one, at the peak of his powers and playing in his own country where he is regarded as a deity and not such a minor one at that.

When MCC left England they were optimistic and were determined to prove the Jonahs wrong. Cowdrey's side was not going to sit back and lose the series. The West Indies were going to have to come to them and beat them. There is a difference and it made for an intriguing situation.

But, as the touring side, MCC had another problem to get over. Whatever country a cricketer plays for, he finds it a different game overseas and this is particularly so when that country is the West Indies. The climate, the wickets, the attitude of the people to the game, the type of cricketers produced, the tempo of life, are all different. In the West Indies, as everywhere else, Test Matches are decided in the middle, but only part of the story of any tour takes place on the field of play. If one is to understand fully the game in another country, it is important to try to understand the character of that country and its people.

In England cricket is a tradition, in the West Indies it is an important and immediate part of life. West Indian spectators, as Englishmen have seen at Lord's and elsewhere, are totally involved in cricket with their all-or-nothing temperaments. In the Caribbean at Test Match time life stops. The shops are short-handed, transistors blare continuously, the bar waiters may well spill your drink over you as he hurries to get back for the first ball of the next over. People tell each other the score all the time and nothing else matters. For each one of the eleven who represent the West Indies in a Test Match there are many thousands just as passionately and ambitiously involved. There may be 25,000 people at a Test Match in Port of Spain, but there are no spectators: just 25,022 participants.

Everywhere I went cricket was being played by waiters at the back of the hotels, by children on the road, and by children and adults on any other open piece of ground, however rough. They played in Montego Bay, in Kingston, in Castries, in Bridgetown, in Port of Spain, and in Georgetown. In Jamaica cricket is tempered by tourism and tartan Bermuda shorts, and in Trinidad it has to share with Carnival and oil production, although during a Test Match every employee has to be given two half-days, which ensures that oil will never reign supreme. In St. Lucia they play cricket and speak in a French dialect and in Guyana, which is the West Indies and South America rolled into one, the game fights its way through internal racial and political troubles. But in Barbados, which is the most relaxed of all the islands, cricket is a reason for living and it has no challengers, not even the sugar production.

One day during the last fortnight of the tour in Georgetown I walked down Main Street from my hotel to the Sea Wall, where the water is a dirty brown colour and the sand is muddy. As I was looking out to sea a car drew up and four children jumped out with a cricket bat and three empty beer bottles. They ran onto the sand and set up the bottles and marked out a wicket. One boy got ready to bat, one to bowl, one to keep wicket, and the other to field at extra-cover. Then they started. The batsman settled over his bat, the wicket-keeper crouched down, and the bowler ran in and bowled. The batsman played an off-drive and the fielder gave chase. He had run three runs by the time the fielder had dropped his hand down on the sand and straightened up and thrown. But there was no ball: it was all mime. The show continued for ten minutes with the children having a marvellous time. I waited in the hope that someone would be out, but before this could happen the car returned and the boys picked up the bottles and piled back in. This little scene showed me, more than anything else I saw, what cricket means to the West Indians.

It is easy to see the West Indies through a cloud of tourist culture and therefore, in a way, not to see the West Indies at all. Life in luxurious surroundings is easy to enjoy and in the expensive hotels in the Caribbean one can soon become submerged by the US dollar and the American accent. No one spends a month in a hotel on the North Coast of Jamaica without getting a suntan, but few people learn much about the island or the people. The syndicates have poured money into the hotels so as to extract the last dollar out of American tourists, who are provided with effortless and instant West Indies.

Calypsos and limbo dances are laid on unceasingly. 'Jamaica Farewell' is sung in Jamaica, Barbados, and St. Lucia, and probably in Guadeloupe and Martinique as well. Hotel prices are quoted in US dollars, plastic palm trees can be bought as souvenirs, Bermuda shorts are sold by the gross, and all the taxi drivers know the way to the nearest night club. The West Indian way of life has a struggle to emerge through all this. But rum does, and so does cricket.

In the cricketing sense the West Indies is a generic name for four independent countries set as much as fifteen hundred miles apart. Three are islands—Jamaica, Trinidad and Barbados—the fourth, Guyana, is part of the South American continent, and two dependant groups of islands, The Windwards and The Leewards. The four countries are very different. Jamaica and Barbados are tourist centres, Trinidad is an industrial island, while Guyana is still searching for a sense of national identity. The people in each country are different. In all of them the descendants of African slaves form the majority of the population, and although their general characteristics are similar, they have acquired the individual traits of the countries in which they live.

Trinidad has one of the most cosmopolitan communities in the world, and the various nationalities have mixed to produce an exciting people who are unmistakeably Trinidadian. The French Roman Catholics, who at the beginning of the nineteenth century outnumbered the ruling Spaniards, influenced the development of Carnival, which has become the most colourful Mardi Gras festival in the world. The Carnival season runs from Christmas to Ash Wednesday and in general the people of Trinidad are as colourful as the festival.

Barbados is a quieter island. Tourism flourishes on the white beaches of the West Coast, and the rest of the island is given over to growing sugar. Industry has hardly gained a foothold. Barbados was never anything but English and the steady influence of the colonists has produced a coloured population that is less volatile than in the other countries. Barbados is the only one of the main cricket centres where rioting has never taken place during a Test Match, and although Africans are by nature a gay, excitable people, it will be surprising if they riot in Barbados because they have been conditioned to a calmer way of life there.

Jamaica is in a way two countries in one. The North Coast is a playground for the rich and has a rather hollow atmosphere. The rest of the island is very poor and in the South, Kingston acts like a magnet to Jamaicans living in the rural areas. It is characterised by a high level of unemployment, poor education, an element of Voodoo, the Rastafarian sect, and general discontent. Crime flourishes, some taxi drivers carry loaded guns, and it was here that the spectators rioted during the Second Test. Not surprisingly, in Kingston the coloured Jamaicans are uncertain and suspicious.

In Georgetown, Guyana is the West Indies, but a mile outside it becomes South America. When I said goodbye to the maid who looked after me in the Park Hotel, she smiled at me and said, "All good things come to an end, yes, I hope so," in a delightfully West Indian way; Sparrow's Calypso Spectacular could not have had a more excitable and enthusiastic audience. The same country boasts the tallest waterfall in the world—the Kaiteur falls. Indigenous tribes hunt with bows and arrows and blow-pipes and do not know what cricket is. They live in Amazon country which is both impressive and beautiful, and their greatest problem is trying to stop the missionaries altering their way of life. Back in Georgetown and in the fertile belt of land near the coast, the Africans are just outnumbered by the Indians, who were brought to British Guiana as indentured labour after emancipation. The two races despise each other and at election time support different parties and frequently fight.

Each country has its charm as well as its drawbacks, but I found the people I met in every island, in the streets and in the rum shops, were friendly and always interested in cricket. Cricket was the one important common thread, and rum too, though each of these four countries have their own brand: Mount Gay in Barbados, Appleton's in Jamaica, Fernandez in Trinidad, and D'A rum in Guyana.

The slaves were emancipated in the West Indies in the 1830's, and it was only then that a large part of the population was free to start developing its own culture. It was also around this time that the English colonists brought cricket to the West Indies. Cricket is therefore one of their oldest traditions. It suits their temperaments and so has become their national game. Since those days there has never been any need for an opinion poll to gauge its popularity or for the authorities to change the rules. It may seem strange that the volatile West Indians should have taken to cricket when so many faster and more dramatic games exist. The aspect of the game they seem to enjoy most of all is the element of personal combat. There is no spectacle a West

Indian crowd enjoys more than a batsman ducking at the last moment to avoid a bumper, except when he stands up and hooks it for six.

The MCC party were going to have to play cricket for three and a half months in front of crowds which would without exception produce an atmosphere of colourful excitement and in the main be appreciative of what they saw. At the same time it was perhaps logical that victory or defeat would mean rather more to the Jamaican and the Guyanese crowds than to the Barbados crowd. But the MCC were also going to play cricket in countries which, although collected under one name, were very different in so many ways, each with its own complex of problems.

2

Carnival and calypso

Trinidad is the most exciting of the cricket islands. It is the island of the three Cs, three from Cricket, Carnival, Crumpet, and Calypso. The girls are beautiful; Calypso, which began in Trinidad, is one of the most compulsive rhythms of all; the feeling for cricket is intense; and Carnival, a unique pre-Lenten festival, focuses the mood of a gay, spontaneous people in forty-eight hours of continual feting (pronounced fetting in Trinidad) at the end of February.

In the islands of sun, sand, and tourism, part of the atmosphere is inevitably artificially created, but few tourists go to Trinidad, so the people are not trying to "sell" the island or themselves. It is an industrial island with its own individual atmosphere, which has not been influenced by the demands of tourism and the dollar. What there is in Trinidad is natural—and there is a lot. Port of Spain is one of the most cosmopolitan cities in the world. The original indigenous inhabitants, the Amerindians, are extinct, but they have left their mark on the island. Many of the names of places and even of various foods are Amerindian. Many races have followed the Amerindians into Trinidad—Spanish, Portuguese, French, English, Chinese, Indians, and others. All have contributed to the development of the island's culture.

These different races have not curtained themselves off and continued to live as one with their own traditions and culture. They have integrated together to produce a new culture that is Trinidad's own. At any big gathering it would need more than an atlas to divide the mixtures into nationalities, but each nationality as it has come to Trinidad has blended into the island and had some influence on its development. The people themselves have developed into Trinidadians.

The faces round the exit at Piarco Airport, which is about twenty miles from Port of Spain, showed signs of some twenty different nationalities. A Seikh chauffeur called Jit

Singh drove me in his almost new Zodiac into Port of Spain and talked knowledgeably about the island. When I asked him if the girls in Trinidad were as beautiful as they were said to be, he shrugged his shoulders and said: "I like girls. I have many girl friends," and changed the subject.

After Barbados the roads in Trinidad were spectacular. They were wide and straight and not only was 70 mph a realistic speed, but the taxi went at 70 without sounding as if it was going to fall apart. As we drove, the mountains we had just flown over stood in the middle distance on the right in a haze of sunlight and clouds. None of them was more than 2,500 to 3,000 feet tall, but mountains help a countryside as a frame helps a picture. The land stretching up to them was flat, and the sugar cane swayed in the wind with an inevitable boredom.

Driving through a new country for the first time is exciting and although the scenery on this journey was dull compared to many others in the West Indies, the countryside had character. We passed a big road going off to the left towards San Fernando and the oilfields at Pointe-a-Pierre and beyond, and all the time the traffic moved at a brisk pace. The sign pointing to the West Indian Tobacco Company went by on the right and further on towards the outskirts of Port of Spain we passed the Angostura Company. The world's supply of Angostura bitters comes from Trinidad and its recipe has always remained the closely guarded secret of the Company. We were held up by the traffic at the docks and Jit Singh asked me if I was there for the Carnival. Then came Independence Square where every building seemed to be Barclays DCO, every waiting car a taxi, and every pedestrian in a hurry. On down Frederick Street, crammed with small shops, and then, after turning three more right-angles, we came to the Savannah.

The Savannah is to Port of Spain what Hyde Park is to London, but more so. It is a vast area of grassland in the middle of Port of Spain. It may be two, three, or four times as big as Hyde Park. The race course, which must be one of the most beautiful in the world, is in the middle and on the hundreds of acres of grass countless cricket matches are played. Over on the right, the Trinidad Hilton rises out of the foliage on the side of the hill. The flagpole of the Governor General's house sticks out of more trees on the other side. One evening, in the far left corner in a small dip in the ground, some steel bands were playing in preparation for Carnival, watched by thousands of spectators. The Savannah was a wonderful place for walking and observing. And the mountains look down on the Savannah.

At the nearby Queens Park Hotel the car door was opened by an elderly, distinguished porter who had a strong touch of Chinese about him, and he led me up the wide steps into a spacious colonial hall. The white Trinidadian girl smiled elegantly as I signed the register. A delightful African took me into the lift, which started and stopped and started again, and he grinned at me and told me that "Mister Graveney and Mister Cowdrey" were good, but not good enough.

I went outside later in the day and no one tried to "sell" me "sights" or night clubs or restaurants or anything else. I walked back some of the way we had driven that morning. Near the Savannah I was in a fairly well-to-do residential area. The small houses were neat and well cared for, and the tiny gardens, which were a mass of exciting colours, were carefully looked after. The trees and shrubs provided plenty of greenery and as the road was small, there was only the occasional car to spoil the peace. Every few yards there were groups of tiny children playing in the gardens or on the pavement and occasionally a bigger child would come tearing round the corner on a bicycle. When I passed anyone, young or old, I smiled and said "good afternoon", and they smiled and wished me one back. It was a natural response. The children looked up and shouted it out through a mouthful of white teeth, the women said it prettily, bowing their heads as they spoke, and the men said it and smiled and kept walking. It was an afternoon scene such as one might find anywhere, but the people I talked to were unselfconsciously friendly.

At the bottom of this road was a cemetery full of ornate gravestones and as I went on the gardens became smaller and the houses became poorer wooden bungalows, many of them opening onto the street. But they were still as carefully kept. Most of the houses had their front doors open and I could see highly polished brass jugs or ornaments on small tables or shelves, just as there are in many English houses of elderly working-class people. They were obviously a source of pride to the owners as they were in a position where anyone who looked into the house would see them.

At one street corner there was a small chemist's shop and I went inside to buy some aspirin. When I told the old woman behind the counter that I had a headache she was concerned and suggested that I should buy many other things besides aspirins which she thought were better. She seemed genuinely worried that aspirin would not be enough. We talked for a while and when she gave me my change she insisted on shaking my hand and she wished me a happy visit.

As I walked back the shops and offices were closing and I was passed by several young men in well-pressed suits hurrying to the bus stops. Some girls, also from the shops, dressed mostly in neat dark skirts with white shirts, flitted past chattering happily to each other. It was a cheerful every day scene.

Carnival was a bare six weeks away and the excitement and expectation it produces in the entire population is remarkable. Carnival takes place each year on the two days before Ash Wednesday and it dates back to the early nineteenth century when the French immigrants shaped its development, but all the nationalities mixed together in Trinidad have left their mark. The Festival was originated by the slaves, who celebrated sugar cane "crop over" with fires lit from burning cane, "cannes brulees" and the slaves also imitated their rulers by disguising themselves to look like them.

Proceedings begin at five o'clock on the Monday morning with "J'Ouvert," the break of day, and end with "Las Lap" at midnight on the Tuesday. Tens of thousands of people in Port of Spain and the other towns dance and fête through the streets with an apparently inexhaustible supply of energy to the bands of the masqueraders. And there are over a hundred bands. "Band" describes any group of masqueraders under one leader and not just the instrumentalists alone. One "band" can number more than two thousand people.

The bands portray in their get-ups an enormous variety of human activity. They may represent periods of history, the world of fantasy, the people of other countries in the past, the present, or the future, in authentic or imaginary presentations. Once a band-leader has decided on the theme for his band all his followers dress themselves accordingly. The costumes are magnificent and involve enormous preparation and expense. The leaders decide on their theme for the next year soon after Carnival has ended. The new costumes have to be decided upon and made up through the following year. The importance of Carnival to the Trinidadians is shown by the fact that the ordinary masquerader, who merely follows the band of his choice through the streets, is willing to spend so much time and money in preparing for these two days and when Carnival is over men even go to prison for not being able to pay their debts.

The 1968 Carnival saw a tremendous range of ideas. Festival of the Inca, Primeval Rites of Spring, Nagas of Assam, Liberation of France, Land of the Xhymers, Conquest of Hannibal the Great, Oriental Fantasy, El Dorado, City of Gold, Brazilian Fiesta, Court of Dionysus, Conquerors of Ninevah, Pageantry of Vikings, were the titles of some of the bands.

The Trinidadians live for Carnival, and at Carnival time all inhibitions disappear. The bands go through the streets where they like, for two days cars stop running in the main part of the city, and people are themselves as they dance and shuffle rhythmically behind their favourite band, snatching a glass or a sandwich from onlookers as they go. The cabinet minister and the maid are equal. Everyone dances with everyone else.

Before the two days of Carnival there is a period while Port of Spain warms up. I was there early in January and the pre-Carnival atmosphere was thick. I had not been in Port of Spain more than a day before at least fifteen people had said to me, "Are you here for Carnival? You can't leave Trinidad without seeing Carnival. You must come back for Carnival." Everyone all the time. I began to wonder how the First Test Match fitted into all this.

When I went to the Portuguese Club I discovered. On my third day in Trinidad I was interviewed on their version of *Woman's Hour*, which was better named as *Listen Ladies*. I talked authoritatively about fashions in King's Road, Chelsea, and the advantages and maybe disadvantages of mini-skirts and maxi-skirts. The compère of the programme, Lillian

Fraser, promised to show me some of the preparations for Carnival, and one evening after dinner she took me to the Portuguese Club to see the Jump-Up, the main Carnival dance.

As we got out of the taxi on the east side of the Savannah over a hundred yards from the club, the calypso beat hit me. Inside the small hall the noise was deafening, but the effect was exhilarating. About 150 closely packed people were vibrating round the room, swaying from foot to foot. The entire place throbbed to the beat and it was a picture of complete freedom. There is no style of dancing. After a time you get the feel of the music and the atmosphere and the rhythm, and then you go with it as if it has seeped into your body and taken charge. The West Indians are wonderful dancers. They move lightly on their feet, their balance is good, and above all they have an inbuilt sense of rhythm. When a West Indian dances it is almost as if he is part of the band, because he moves so completely with the rhythm of the music. In this crowded room the dancers were all totally involved; they moved naturally, not looking at their feet or their hands but up in the air as if they were feeling the music. They give an impression of movement but in fact they hardly move at all. Their hips are going all the time and most West Indian men have small hips, which exaggerates the movement. They use their hands but the feet movements are not extravagant. Everything is smoothly co-ordinated. I only realised how naturally graceful and economical their dancing was when I saw some English visitors trying to do the same. Each man and girl was dancing in his or her own way. There was nothing to conform to except the rhythm, and each person conformed to this as he wanted. Some gyrated opposite each other, some danced sideways on with their arms around each other's waists, and some just stood where they were and "beat" with their hips. Nothing mattered; race, age, colour, or creed.

Sometimes the men put their hands above their heads, then swing them down by their sides and backwards, as if to emphasise one particular beat. They did not do this together but when they felt like it. The girls were less demonstrative, although they moved just as well. Some were in purple, some in sleeveless tops and trousers, some in gay micro-skirts, and two in bright green trouser-suits. They were all attractive, with fine complexions, and a lot of them had that strong hair, fair or dark, which grows long and looks right. The men wore trousers and open-necked shirts. All were lost in the rhythm, caught up in a compulsive freedom, sweat glistening on their faces as they craved for the next beat and were ready for it when it came. This was the 'Jump-Up'.

The band-leader was Wayne Berkeley. Wayne was not playing himself that night. As I was introduced to him he gripped my hand eagerly, asked me what I wanted to drink, and went through to the bar to get me a Scotch. He handed me the glass and as we stood by the door people kept rushing past and there was a constant ring of "Will you win? You must win. You'll win, Wayne." Victory in the parade of bands at Carnival is a great triumph. "Hullo," a girl cried out from behind him. As he turned she kissed him, throwing her arms around his back. Wayne turned back to me.

"I think she was here the other night," he said. It did not matter who anyone was.

When Lillian Fraser told him I was travelling with the MCC he looked serious.

"Why are you doing so badly?" He frowned and when I did not answer immediately he went on, "I'll tell you what the matter is . . . " Carnival was forgotten, cricket took over, theories were produced, and everyone within earshot joined in. For almost a quarter of an hour it was cricket and only cricket. We went through the English side and the West Indian side and it was not just stupid chatter. A lot of sense was talked. Then Wayne shouted a name in my ear and I looked up into a smiling Chinese face.

"I am the only English band-leader in Trinidad," he laughed. "I was born in London. Will you win the Test Match?" And there was a chorus of "no" and then a lot of laughter. Suddenly the band stopped playing and someone had a hurried conversation with Wayne. It was back to Jump-Up and Carnival. I left at half-past three and people were still coming. I am sure it was going strong at half-past six. And Carnival was six weeks away.

The Trinidadians are uninhibited. They were being themselves at the Portuguese Club. They were being themselves after tea on the last day of the First Test when, as

Wes Hall played his formidable forward defensive stroke, a group of spectators began to sing, 'Fire in your Wire', Calypso Rose's 1967 Carnival success.

So much of what is looked upon as West Indian culture belongs to Trinidad. The calypso, the steel band, and the limbo dance all originated and developed in Trinidad, and the people are proud of it. When they are sung, played, and danced in Trinidad they have a verve about them that is missing in the other islands. The calypso is the most exciting of the three.

The West Indians talk and sing as rhythmically as they dance, and they have a great ability to rhyme. When I was in a restaurant or sitting round a bar, a group of two or three guitar players would sometimes come up and sing a calypso about me or the people I was with. They would make up the words as they went along and somehow fit them in. When the West Indians sing like this they seem to be able to make words as different as egg and holiday rhyme together. However, I did not come across this type of calypso-singing in Trinidad, but only in the tourist islands—particularly in Jamaica. It is remarkable what they can do with their tuneful voices, but groups of three guitar players and an American audience do not catch the atmosphere or the meaning of the Trinidadian calypso.

Calypsos are written about almost anything, from topical events and scandals to Expo '67 and bikinis, from mother-in-laws to Gary Sobers. Cricket is a great favourite for the calypsonians and especially during a Test series. At a show in Bridgetown they sang calypsos about Hall's batting on the last evening of the First Test, which saved the match for the West Indies, and they sang about Graveney's century, about Kanhai and Cowdrey. Nearly all the good calypso-singers come from Trinidad and when the Test Matches were being played in Barbados and Guyana groups of them flew over to give shows. The response was amazing and the atmosphere unforgettable. Most of the calypsos are humorous and the rhythm of both the words and the music is strong. For a visitor, calypsos sung properly are difficult to understand. The lyrics are written in Trinidad English, when "I" becomes "ah" and "your" becomes "you" and "her" becomes "she", and they are sung fast in the Trinidad accent.

The audiences make them even more difficult to understand because they anticipate each joke by half a line.

The West Indians make bad spectators. As with cricket the audience participates, and these calypso shows are more like vast spontaneous parties. Each calypso will bring the audience laughing and shouting to its feet, and when a West Indian audience laughs it does so wholeheartedly. All through the evening people will be turning round in their seats to talk to those behind them and the gangways, which provide the standing room, are also packed. There are even people crouching on the floor in front of the stalls. There is no such thing as formality, or air conditioning either.

Throughout the whole show there are people standing on the stage watching, having nothing to do with the band at all. They are simply friends of someone who has told them they had better go and stand on the stage. The programme frequently gets out of order and the wrong band comes on for the wrong singer. The lights may fuse but no one minds and people just laugh. Many calypsos have a strong bedroom sense of humour which the audience love, and each innuendo, though there were very few references oblique enough to be called innuendoes, sent the theatre into hysterics. Sparrow's 'Steering Wheel' is a gentle example:

> *She tell me no I ain't going Careenage*
> *Stay right here in the garage*
> *I am afraid and you know after hours*
> *Down dey have night prowlers*
> *Anything you have to do, do it here*
> *We ain't have nothing to fear*
> *When ah hold she to demonstrate me plan*
> *Is then the trouble began*
> *CHORUS*
> *She start ah working up, ah working up, ah working up*
> *And she carrying on*
> *She foot stick in the steering wheel*
> *Blowing the bloody horn   Wah*
> *She father come out one hatchet in he hand and the old*
>   *bull start to shout*
> *Shame Sparrow shame*
> *You spoiling me daughter name*

Sparrow don't come back here again you are the one to
　blame
Supposing me daughter strain

Can you imagine this long-legged woman
In such an awkward position
And me the best friend of the family
Couldn't be more guilty
If she did keep she tail quiet nobody
Woulda know the garage had activity
But she kicking up like she mad
Waving she leg like a blasted flag

This time the dog started to bark
Don't talk how the garage dark
Ah start to feel in the dark because ah couldn't see
She bawl he he he you tickling me
Like she big toe hook the indicator
This time she ankle quite in the gear lever
Ah fighting hard to untangle she
But the noise only waking everybody

She little brother and she two nephew
Come outside and peeping too
Ah had to run away from the car
Ah couldn't face the Granmother
This time me jacket flying me shoes in me hand
My pants get away from the mid section
In the dark ah stumble and fall
The dog take me socks underpants and all

There is nothing too complicated about it.

Two of the big competitions at Carnival are to decide the Calypso King and the Road March King. The "Road March" goes to the writer of the tune which is played most on the roads during the two days of Carnival. The "Road March" is the Trinidadian "hit parade" at Carnival time. For the last six years the "Road March" has developed into a straight fight between the two leading calypso singers, The Mighty Sparrow and Lord Kitchener. Kitch is winning easily. In 1968 Kitch's 'Miss Tourist' won with Sparrow's 'Mister Walker' some way behind. They both have good easy tunes and simple catching words, but it is the steel bands who decide which will win, for it is they who play the tunes. Kitch's tunes leave the steel bandsmen more room to fit arrangements of their own into the central melody, and it may be that it is this which brought Kitch the "Road March" title in five years out of six. Sparrow and Kitch are tremendous rivals and no one in Trinidad is indifferent to them. Either Kitch is loved and Sparrow hated, or Kitch hated and Sparrow loved.

Their Carnival rivalry starts well before the two days of the Festival. The Carnival season begins after Christmas up to Easter when there are four or five nightly calypso shows, the calypso tents as they are known, where the new calypsos are sung. Kitch has his own "tent" and so does Sparrow. They produce the same passionate excitement, but they are both very different. Sparrow, whose real name is Slinger Francisco, is more of a showman than Kitch. He is always immaculately dressed, his stage manner is highly polished, and he puts himself across strongly. 'Mister Walker' was certainly a great tune and I found it more catching than 'Miss Tourist'. In the other islands it was better known and in Guyana I heard it on the radio every time I switched it on. Yet 'Miss Tourist' was played more often during Carnival, and was more my idea of a traditional calypso. Kitch's voice is less resonant but slightly gravelly and does not have to rely so much on the tune. His presentation is less spectacular than Sparrow's and although at first he is not so easy to listen to, there is something about his voice which is remote and therefore effective. He has won the "Road March" so often that he must have something which appeals particularly to Trinidadian ears. Sparrow told me that he thought 'Miss Tourist' won because it was played more often on the stage, for which it was better suited, while 'Mister Walker', a marching tune, went better on the road.

Calypso goes on developing. It may be that Sparrow's sound is something which is still arriving, and Carnival dances develop in the same way. In recent years the 'Jump-Up', the 'beak-away', 'fireman', 'saga ting', and 'rocking the ship' have all become recognised Carnival dances. They are without set pattern and some are fast and some slow. Carnival may be the big moment of the year, but Port of Spain does not go to sleep for the other 363 days. A people who can produce Carnival and all its trappings could never be dull.

"M" was another interesting letter in Trinidad. It stood for Maracas Bay, with its lovely beach about twenty miles out of Port of Spain, and the Miramar, a night club. Here the taxi dropped me and I walked up two concrete steps, through a big door, and up a wide flight of dimly lit stairs. The only light came from a bulb at the top by the desk. There were three men standing round it and a girl sitting behind. They looked suspiciously at me as I climbed up but when I mentioned MCC they smiled and showed me to the door on the right.

This led to a big room with a square dance-floor raised like a boxing-ring in the middle. Through the haze, I could see three couples dancing, two like sparring partners and the third like heavyweights just before the referee shouts "break". I walked slowly towards the ring down a pathway between the bare tables and wooden chairs. There were several people standing between the ring and the bar, and there were a few couples sitting at the tables. I walked to the bar and the talk stopped momentarily while I was scanned. I bought the usual rum and coke and sat down at the side of the dancing dais. Those that had looked at me as I came in had now forgotten about me and were talking amongst themselves. It was a night club for the locals and for the sailors. There were no visitors there and when, later on, two middle-aged American men came in, they too were scrutinised.

I was sitting with my back to the bar and to a passage beside the bar which probably led to the lavatories. Some girls dressed in vivid colours were standing around behind me talking. They were the usual Trinidad mixture of nationalities and in the dim light some were very striking. Those of African descent had round faces while those with predominantly Portuguese or Spanish blood had narrow faces with sharply etched features. Several men were hanging about them, for the girls were eager for their charms to be appreciated. But they knew most of the men and I never heard terms being discussed, and they never tried to persuade me. Some of the men were Trinidadians and others had come off the ships in the harbour and spoke a variety of languages.

There was an attractive girl with red hair, wearing a bright chequered trouser-suit who went onto the floor with a fair-haired man with a strong Nordic look about him. They danced magnificently for a long time and without saying a word to each other. The band was playing loudly on a raised platform on the far side of the room, but the room was big enough to absorb the noise. As the band went from quick to slow these two went with it, their hips showing the way. The air was heavy with smoke and in such down-to-earth circumstances they made a marvellous sight. I watched them for a long time, throwing my finished cigarettes onto the wooden floor and stamping them out, and then the two Americans came in and sat down at a table on the other side of the dance-floor. They had obviously been told that they should go to the Miramar to see "life", and for several minutes they talked rapidly with their heads together and every now and then one of them looked quickly round the room. They ordered some Scotch and had some trouble finding the right amount of money to pay for it.

After three more Scotches they began to look anxiously at the girls and then back at each other, as they tried to pluck up courage to ask them to dance. Eventually they did so and had to walk all the way round to where I was sitting to get onto the floor, since there was only one entrance. For five minutes they sweated to try and find a step which would suit them. The girls were fine dancers and made both men look ridiculous, although exuding the brash self-confidence of American tourists, they appeared not to notice it. When they stopped dancing the girls walked quickly back down the passage while the men called for some more Scotch.

I was sitting and taking everything in when I felt a thump on my left side and a sailor in uniform who was very drunk lurched into the chair beside me. He tried to talk, but his words like his movements were slurred; then he suddenly belched loud and long before spitting forcibly onto the floor. He reached over and took a cigarette from my packet and the bar waiter caught my eye and smiled. I ordered myself another drink and when it came this sailor snatched it and downed it in one. I ordered another and sat somewhere else.

The floor filled up as more people came into the club. I watched a small man with an ample tummy who must have been well into his sixties walk on followed by a well-built woman in a black dress who could not have been much younger. He was wearing a red check shirt which hung loosely down outside a pair of light cotton trousers and he had a dark green homburg perched on his head in the West Indian way which is neither quite on the back nor on the front. The two of them danced for more than half an hour. They stood apart and moved in their own economical way to the calypso beat. The sailors and their girls may have been more energetic, but they were certainly no more rhythmical. The homburg hat and the smile stayed in place. If the man had been an Englishman he might have been a porter at Smithfield Market or maybe a taxi driver. When he led his wife off the floor he saw me looking and his smile broadened. "Man, that was fun," he said. They were back on the floor within fifteen minutes.

I left at half-past one. When I walked onto the pavement a man stuck his head out of a car window and shouted, "taxi". My hotel was not too far away and so I shook my head and continued walking. The taxi driver shouted something after me which I did not hear. I had walked about thirty yards when a car drew up beside me.

"It's alright, thank you, I'm going to walk home," I said.

"I know sir, but it is not safe at this time," came the answer.

I was sure that the driver was doing all that he could to con a fare when a policeman came up.

"He says he going to walk home and ah tell him it's not safe," said the driver.

The policeman looked at me.

"Man," he said, "you get inside. It is not safe."

Of course Trinidad is not Carnival, Calypso and uninhibited enjoyment all the time and it is not quite so naive and uncomplicated as it seems at Carnival time. It is not safe to walk in the streets at night in the middle of Port of Spain. When England were winning the Test Match there on the 1959/60 tour the crowd, annoyed by an umpiring decision which went against the West Indies, threw bottles and stopped the match.

Wayne Berkeley showed me how cricket fitted into the life of Trinidad and what the game means to the people and Queen's Park Oval is by a long way the most beautiful ground in the West Indies. This first Test which saw cricket as a game of elegance and grandeur could not have found a finer setting.

3

The grandeur of cricket

An hour before the start on the first day, the Queen's Park Oval was an unforgettable sight. The gates had been open since seven o'clock and still there were long chattering queues outside. Inside, the excitement and suspense were extreme. Already more than twenty thousand people were in position, talking, gesticulating, and waiting. It was a colourful crowd. There were flashes of red and orange and green and purple; the girls wore the brightest colours, and if the men were more soberly dressed, their flashing white teeth told of their mood. The sun was hot, and coloured umbrellas were held aloft to keep off the heat. The nut-vendor on the far side, in his scarlet coat and hat, was doing great business in the stands and there were already four men sitting on the branches of a tree overlooking the ground. I caught the eye of a man near the Press box and he shouted, "you see Wes and Charlie", and there was a great roar of laughter from everyone around. MCC had done badly so far on this tour and no one gave much for England's chances, least of all the Trinidadians.

The groundstaff had given the wicket its final delicate touches and it now lay under the sun like some gastronomic delight on a dish, waiting to be served. Meanwhile players and officials were prodding and admiring it. The crescendo of the expectant chatter from the ring gave it all a gladiatorial atmosphere. It was not going to be a day or a match for weak hearts.

The atmosphere in the ground was in sharp contrast to the atmosphere surrounding it. The mountains on the north side give the Queen's Park Oval a quiet reflective beauty. The highest rises to no more than two and a half thousand feet, but they are closely wooded right to the summit. The dark green of the trees was broken at intervals by large patches of yellowy-green grass which had enjoyed the last rain but was just beginning to need some more. The colour contrasts were heightened by the clouds which seldom leave these hills. As they flit past overhead, one patch of hillside is plunged into dark shadow just as suddenly as another is illuminated by the bright sunlight. It is a scene which I watched for nine days and it improved all the time. There are no tall blocks of flats or towers of industry to mar this setting: just a few quite pleasant English colonial gables.

The stands themselves are very modern and a vast new double-decker was being used for the first time during the Test Match. No one was quite certain what a capacity crowd was; some said 28,000 and some even more, but it was probably rather less. The gates were shut an hour after the start on the first day and yet the official attendance figure was given as less than 22,000 so either there was an illicit way in or there was less room than the optimists forecasted.

These stands are overlooked at well-spaced intervals by impressive-looking Samaan trees. From a big trunk these trees burst out into a thick, light green foliage and look like vast spreading mushrooms. They help the friendly atmosphere of this ground. There is also a group of three palm trees over deep mid-off and they add their own shade of green.

It is a setting of complete serenity which the turmoil inside does nothing to disturb, though it makes cricket a difficult game for the nervous. The crowd is a vital part of any West Indian Test Match. At Queen's Park Oval every ball, every stroke, every incident, humorous or serious, brought a response. No bumper was bowled without a roar coming from the crowd, and a hook for four proved just as stimulating. When the English were batting an appeal for lbw or a catch at the wicket, or even a batsman playing and missing, brought thousands to their feet. The men shouted, cupping one hand round their mouths to make sure their advice carried and shaking the other in the air to make their point more definite. They were, too, an appreciative crowd. A glorious stroke no matter from whom was loudly praised, but a ferocious six brought the house down and then the noise lasted for the next two or three balls.

To add to the din came the noise from the transistors, turned well up. So the crowd learnt that the batsman had to play an inswinging yorker at about the same time as the batsman himself. Fun for everyone, except possibly the batsman. But they were a fair crowd and both sides got their share of the praise and the blame. Advice was given all the time and for nothing, and the fielder on the boundary received a thorough lesson in all the arts of the game. Graveney's innings in the First Test will be talked about for a long time in Port of Spain and so will Lloyd's, but Lloyd's will be talked about just a little bit louder. And it would be unnatural for any crowd not to be partisan. For a batsman coming out to bat for the first time, these circumstances can be very trying.

Queen's Park Oval is surely a setting for great deeds, and appropriately there could not have been a much better Test Match than the first. For five days it saw cricket at its best. During the first two and a bit England built up a big advantage and forced the West Indies to spend the rest of the time trying to save the match. This may sound too one-sided to make for a great cricket match, but it had everything in it that cricket is all about.

In mid-afternoon on the fourth day, in one of those inexplicable collapses, the West Indies lost their last six wickets for a mere 73, and failed to save the follow-on by six runs. England now had one full day of five and a half hours and 110 minutes that night to bowl them out again, but no sooner had Cowdrey invited Sobers to bat again than a fierce storm flooded the ground. So much for the 110 minutes and presumably with them, England's chances. An hour after lunch on the final day the West Indies were going comfortably along at 164 for 2 on a wicket which was playing as easily as at any time in the match. Sixty minutes later when they went into tea the same scoreboard read 180 for 8. It was an astonishing collapse by a fine batting side which had collectively lost its nerve. There was no other reason. In an hour an almost certain English victory had appeared from nowhere. As the Englishmen came off the field they were looking at each other with dazed smiles as if the whole thing was a conjuring trick. Two hours later they may have felt that it was.

After tea the game took its last dramatic turn. The straight bats and cool heads of Sobers and Hall frustrated all Cowdrey's bowling changes. During tea someone must have tempted Providence because she did not retake the field with the Englishmen. Anyway these two steered the West Indies through to a draw. Cricket is the only game where situations change so dramatically and so completely and then go back on themselves so soon afterwards.

In this exciting framework there was plenty of magnificent cricket. Brilliant individual performances were sharply etched by the fierce spirit of challenge. Fascinating duels developed between batsman and bowler and there were those agonising lost opportunities which are a part of every game of cricket ever played. The captains had to make some difficult decisions. There was nothing in most of them at the time, but because of the nearness of the result they acquired new significance later, and with the advantage of hindsight they might have done otherwise. Above all there was an innings of sheer glory by Graveney which lifted cricket back onto Mount Olympus. Batting as was displayed by Graveney that day becomes an art form to rank with the highest.

To see Graveney uncoil himself and his bat time after time in the gentle rhythmical movement of an off-drive is like seeing 'Swan Lake' performed in Heaven. A photographer cannot capture Graveney. The beauty of his batting lies not in any one movement at any one time, but in the sum total of all his movements. He is incapable of playing an ugly shot and his style has developed to allow him to use the full 360 degrees. Stylish movement being artistic and cricket being a game which enables a batsman to play the ball through any angle, from long-stop all the way round to long-stop, Graveney's range is therefore limitless and never wholly repetitious. This makes it such an exciting visual art. In all other games opportunity for artistic movement is limited to a smaller angle and the player can only express himself very subjectively. The scope of cricket is so wide that the batsman has more or less unlimited freedom and Graveney, because of his style, has used this freedom to produce something artistic and beautiful. No art gallery in the world would have turned away his innings that day at Queen's Park Oval.

A cricket match which developed like this one over five days cannot be centred around one individual performance. It was a thrilling contest which had everything, including a crowd which turned excitement into frenzy. Yet Graveney's innings was above everything else that happened, almost a game of cricket on its own.

At forty Graveney is the supreme artist. All batsmen have ways of walking to the crease, but few of them are noticed until they are taking guard. One only has to see Graveney trot down the last three pavilion steps and take his first three strides onto the field to sit up. There is an elegance in his long, even step and angular appearance and, when on his way he looks around the ground, it is as if he is casually noting where he can stroke the ball for four. Some batsmen look furtively around as if they are marking the place for a scurried short single. Graveney has a more expansive look round.

At the crease he stands correct and still, quite relaxed and yet totally alert. Now he prepared to face the third over of the second day with England 244 for 3. Sobers, knowing that another wicket would ruin a lot of the advantage England had built up on the first day, stationed eight fielders for the close catch. There was still some shine left on the new ball. In his own time Graveney surveyed the field and settled over his bat. Griffith came pounding in six times and each time Graveney played the ball in the middle of the bat with time to spare. It was a maiden, but a meaningful maiden. A single by Barrington took Graveney to the other end to face Sobers, bowling fast left-arm over. The first ball was well up to him, Graveney lent on it, and mid-on was trotting back to the sightscreen to fetch it.

Then Hall, all arms and legs, reached the bowling crease and Graveney turned him off his toes through mid-wicket to the boundary. The shot seemed to say, almost apologetically, "that wasn't very fast, you know." Hall got the message. He walked back forty-four paces, turned, hitched up his trousers, and came tearing in again. It was a bouncer. Graveney, in no hurry, hooked and the ball hit the boundary ten yards in front of square-leg, which shows that some forty-year-olds have quick reflexes. In his next over Hall overpitched and was persuaded through extra-cover, and when Holford pitched short he was late-cut in turn. And on it went. It was so easy, so assured, and so elegant. Barrington's difficulties at the other end only etched the innings more clearly.

Graveney's style is copybook. His long experience has welded it into place and taken off any rough edges there may once have been. Technically he is about the best equipped batsman alive. It is difficult to find one specific skill which separates him from other batsmen; rather, it is the sum total of all his skills. He is a very certain judge of length, and quick to spot the extra inch or two which makes the difference between a drive and a forward defensive shot. One of the interesting points about this innings was that Graveney had been having trouble getting used to the light in the early matches, and this had been most noticeable in his judgment of length. He had been playing back when he should have been forward and often his feet had been in the wrong position, something which has hardly ever happened to him. He was not alone in this and in the first three weeks of the tour all the batsmen had spent a lot of time in the nets and on the golf course trying to accustom themselves to the strong light.

By his own standards he had been playing badly in the early matches, but now, quite suddenly and for no reason except that practice helps, all his old certainty returned. All through the match the wicket was a slow turner and ironically, as England won the toss which was so important, it was probably at its worst on the first day. When Graveney was in, Gibbs had a long bowl and was turning his off-breaks a certain amount. He was using all his clever variations of flight and pace which his action conceals so well, yet Graveney was never in a moment's doubt. He played forward or back and was never left stuttering half way on the edge of the popping crease. Like the scoring strokes every defensive shot was deliberate and controlled. Graveney's balance is perfect and this, together with his technique, makes him a fine player of the turning ball.

The crowd were appreciative of this innings too. It was not an impulsive West Indian innings to bring them shouting to their feet, but they seemed to sense what they were watching and they watched carefully. When at last Graveney was bowled, the victim of exhaustion, he walked in to a tremendous reception. Port of Spain will not forget him for a long time. "Man, you see Graveney?" was the start of many conversations over the next few days. Even the taxi drivers, who in Port of Spain, as in most other cities in the world, know everything and are alternately hateful and splendid, grudgingly admitted that it was a good innings and then changed the subject. A Chinese taxi driver put me right over the question of whether or not Cowdrey should have taken the new ball when he did. He was a tiny little man who drove an enormous shining Cadillac with automatic gears and power steering. At each corner he spun the wheel with one finger and at the same time turned to me in the back with a glorious Oriental smile all over his face. Then there was the driver who looked like Paul Robeson with a moustache and who was once a left-arm spinner of no ordinary ability. He asked me if I had heard of him and I regretted that I hadn't, so I heard about him then. His list of victims was impressive and some great players had given him good words of encouragement. I asked him why the West Indian selectors had overlooked him. "You see, I was too good," he answered modestly.

Graveney was incomparable that day, but there were three other batsmen who played innings which were as valuable in the context of the match. Cowdrey won the toss which was an important piece of psychological luck; things had been going so badly before this match that if England had had to bat after two days in the field the result could have been fearful. When the toss was won, Hall and Griffith marked out their long runs and prepared to breathe fire at Boycott and Edrich. This was an anxious moment for England, but Hall's first ball was a not-so-fast full-toss which Boycott drove gratefully past mid-on for four.

Griffith and Sobers also started with full-tosses and 30 runs came in the first half hour. Batting in their own distinctive ways, Boycott and Edrich put on 80 for the first wicket. Hall and Griffith were certainly a good deal slower than they had been in England. Hall had been recovering from a car accident and Griffith had been having trouble with his action, and of course they were both two years older. But the wicket was very slow and none of the West Indies side had had any match practice for more than three months. Even Sobers was less than omnipotent. These two did England a great service that morning and, when an hour and a half later the first spinner came on, they were still together.

With white sweat bands on his wrists and a white cravat round his neck to keep the sun off, Boycott looked more like a monk than a Test cricketer, but he was as determined as any Yorkshireman has ever been. His face was set as he walked out, and it remained so to the end. He did not hear the crowd. When Hall bowled him two half-volleys just outside the leg stump he on-drove them both for four. They were handsome strokes, but he did not look particularly pleased and he probably wasn't. He had been taught that half-volleys are meant for hitting to the boundary and he may have thought that he had done no more than he ought. Boycott is an unemotional player and after Holford had hit him on the pad with his googly and appealed, his only reaction was to hit the next two balls to leg for four. Boycott has a wide range of strokes and he used them all, not flippantly but with serious intent.

Edrich was different, but just as effective. He had made a bad start to the tour and to counteract a weakness outside the off stump he had moved over to middle stump guard. He must have felt a lot better after Sobers had bowled him that first full-toss. Edrich is not a fluent batsman and for much of the time he looks awkward at the crease, but he is a very difficult man to get out.

This opening partnership was the acme of concentration and determination, and how well these two qualities served England that morning. Five minutes before lunch Gibbs held one back and Edrich was caught behind the wicket pushing at it. By then 80 runs were on the board.

When Boycott was lbw to a googly, he left as unemotionally as he had arrived. Inside he was furious although he had played as well as anyone could remember. Boycott does not like getting out and certainly not when well set.

In the afternoon Cowdrey took on from Boycott. Batting with complete composure he had an absorbing duel with Gibbs. The ball was turning after only 90 minutes, when Gibbs first came on. He attacks the batsman all the time and now tried everything he knew to dislodge Cowdrey. He was getting enough turn to have three short-legs and for over after over no two successive balls were the same. One was pushed through a little quicker, one pitched invitingly on middle and off and turning into the leg trap, one was thrown up a little higher, the leg-break was thrown in, and then came the away floater.

Gibbs has a deceptively fast movement of his arms as he

delivers the ball which makes these variations difficult to spot. He runs half-a-dozen quick paces on enormously long legs and his stride is as springy as if he is walking on his toes all the time. If Gibbs entered for a dressage test he would be bound to win it.

Certainly Cowdrey had to use all his technical know-how in the afternoon. When he played forward it was with bat tucked in behind his front pad and held with dropped wrists. But he did not often have to use his bat, for Gibbs, pitching on the off stump, was getting too much turn to get an lbw decision in his favour. For most of the time Cowdrey stretched forward and played the ball with his front pad and thigh, keeping his bat as a secondary line of defence in case the ball turned less than he thought. Every now and then Gibbs overpitched and Cowdrey came forward and drove him through the offside with a broad flowing bat. If he pitched short Cowdrey was quick to drop on it with his wrists and steer it wide of slip.

But Gibbs has one weakness. He does not like bowling round the wicket and if he had done so now Cowdrey would have been forced to play the balls he was taking on his pad, as the different angle could have had him lbw. Apart from two overs Gibbs stayed over the wicket and the battle went on without either side getting on top. This was one of the best of the individual pieces of cricket which went to make up this match. It was master technician against master technician.

While all this was happening at one end Barrington was soldiering on like the faithful and consistent retainer he is. Before the Test Barrington had been more out of form than any of the main batsmen and he was not much better now. As soon as he came in Sobers took off Holford, who had been causing plenty of trouble with his googlies, and brought on Griffith. Sobers was playing from memory. Four years before in a Festival game in England, Barrington had withdrawn in protest over Griffith's action and there was plenty of feeling about this. The fielders gathered round and Griffith began to pitch short. Barrington was soon ducking and weaving and the crowd, sensing the extra element of challenge, joined in. The shouting began as Griffith started his run and when he reached the crease it was at a crescendo.

If Barrington's shot was a safe one it died, but otherwise it continued on to the next ball. As this was a slow wicket a number of the intended bouncers did not rise much more than stump high and several times the ball seemed to graze the back of Barrington's neck as he ducked low. The crowd loved it, but Barrington survived.

Sobers' memory was acute enough, but the circumstances were against him. Hall and Griffith were no longer the fearsome pair of four years earlier, and this wicket was very slow. Even so it was a curious decision to take off Holford who had been bowling so well, and the spinners had all along looked the more likely to take wickets. Griffith certainly played on Barrington's mind, but Barrington has spent a large part of his life at the wicket. He may not like the stuff which flies past his ears, but at least he knows something about avoiding it, even if he did once duck to an intended bounder from Hall which hit him smack on the bottom and produced a loud appeal and a war dance from Hall. It cannot have missed by much, either.

Barrington gave an impression of uncomfortable solidity and when the spinners came back there was much more edge than middle to his bat. Sobers, leaning on his haunches at backward short-leg, may well by then have been reflecting on his decision to remove Holford when Barrington first came in. Maybe it caused him to miss two half-chances from Barrington while he was fielding there in addition to one at slip. For Sobers to miss even half-chances was remarkable, but for England to be past 200 for the loss of only two wickets seemed to be nothing short of a miracle.

Cowdrey and Barrington did England proud that day, Cowdrey graceful and certain, Barrington with his jaw stuck out and his instinct for cricket getting him by. Even so he indulged a couple of times in his favourite party trick of reaching milestones with a six. He had made 44 when Gibbs tried two overs round the wicket. In the second Barrington took a quick step and pull-drove him high into the stand at long-on. Gibbs was so disheartened by this that he returned to the other side of the wicket and continued to beat a tattoo on Cowdrey's front pad. Barrington had done England a notable service. The next day Gibbs again had the misfortune to be bowling when Barrington was within reach of a hundred. When Barrington was 99 he threw one up invitingly and someone in the crowd threw the ball back to Butcher at mid-on.

Happiness is seldom more than a fleeting emotion for English cricket supporters and when Cowdrey was out in the first over the next morning, we were all to well aware of what might happen. But out strode Graveney and we soon saw that the best wine had been kept to the end. At 11.35 on the third day England were all out for 568 against the "World Champions". A lot of people thought that Cowdrey should have declared overnight when England were 546 for 7, and 22 runs may have seemed a slender reward for another 35 minutes batting when we were going to need a lot of time to bowl the West Indies out twice. But what was going to happen could not have taken place had he declared.

Small wonder the steps of the Englishmen were springy as they took the field, even though more than two and half days stretched in front of them. That will o' the wisp called form had mysteriously returned. The spectators were mystified too. They had read and been told that this English side was a wash-out. They came to see "Wes and Charlie" tear a great hole in the innings and for "king" Gary to finish it off. They grew quieter as the first two days wore on, but they did not lose their good humour. They were still generous to the England batsmen and the chatter and the smiles went on even if in a more subdued manner. The atmosphere was wonderfully exhilarating.

Aiming at a total of 369 to save the follow-on is a wearying business after spending nearly two and a half days in the field. Early on the West Indies needed some luck against Brown and Jones, who had found inspiration from the England batsmen and were unrecognisable from the bowlers they had been in the early matches. Snicks bisected the slips, Cowdrey missed a very difficult catch at second slip, and D'Oliveira was insistent when he appealed against Nurse for lbw. Through the day Camacho, Nurse, and Butcher were snuffed out in turn. Camacho made a mess of a hook, Nurse drove without getting to the pitch, and Butcher was unequivocally lbw to a ball which came back off the seam. It was tight cricket; nothing was given either way. The bowling was hostile, the batting watchful, and the out-cricket good. It was fascinating to watch, better still to watch through binoculars.

It was into this tense scene that Clive Lloyd, one of cricket's more unlikely looking heroes, walked when West Indies were 124 for 3. He appeared thoughtfully, six foot two inches tall, bespectacled, with slightly stooping shoulders and a long sloping stride, looking as if he was on his way to the chemistry laboratory. For half an hour he peered watchfully through his glasses. At the other end Kanhai, his hair going impressively grey at the edges, was being the very soul of discretion. Then suddenly he lost patience, swept wildly, and missed. Parks and Titmus thought the lbw appeal should be in England's favour but umpire Gosein did not agree. Kanhai went back to careful defence.

The left-handed Lloyd thought he had looked long enough and, like the chemistry student who hopes he has got the mixture right, he proceeded to apply the flame. Titmus bowled him a good length ball on the middle stump. He swung himself round through almost 180 degrees in a desperate sweep and the ball crashed into the boundary at square-leg. The explosion was successful. When Titmus gave one more air he picked his bat up high and the ball soared back over the bowler's head for six. The crowd went wild with delight. They threw their hats in the air and jumped up and down with their hands above their heads. On Lloyd went, playing some fine strokes on both sides of the wicket. He timed the ball beautifully and he hit straight. In the last over of the day the close fielders gathered round but Lloyd was unaware of them. Hobbs bowled a short one and he went back and drove it through extra-cover. The umpires removed the bails and Lloyd withdrew into the pavilion chewing dispassionately and looking at the ground, leaving the rest of us to go to Alice in Wonderland to find out who he really was. He had only made 36, but he had put West Indies on top of England for the first time in the game.

In the third over the next morning he twice drove Brown through the off-side off the back foot. Not many batsmen can play this shot as well as Lloyd, and soon he was past fifty. He hit the ball just as hard as he had done the night before, his strokes were technically right, and his defence was sound, yet there was something curiously matter-of-fact about it all. By the way he moved he gave the impression that it was by chance as much as anything else that his feet got into the right position. Throughout his innings he made the bowlers think there was something to hope for. But he did not let up until he had made 118.

This was a remarkable first Test innings against England. He came in when the West Indies appeared to be slowly sinking, and he saw them back onto rather more than just an even keel, not by introspective pushes and steers, but by boldly picking up his bat and taking the battle to the bowlers. When he had nearly reached his first Test century wickets began to fall at the other end, but he slowed down and stayed there realising his side's needs. And when he was eighth out with the West Indies needing another 17 to save the follow-on, his only show of emotion was a quick thump of his bat against the ground before he departed slowly, chewing.

If the situation had got the better of him in the end, who can wonder? The West Indies needed only 17 to save the follow-on when Jones bowled him a straight ball which he tried to push wide of mid-on. It hit his middle stump. An unnecessary shot maybe, but a very human one. The pressure had been building up around him as wickets fell and now, with only Griffith, Hall, and Gibbs to help him, he was quite literally the West Indies.

People unfamiliar with cricket cannot know the tensions of these moments. A good many thoughts go through the batsman's mind. "I'll go on as I am and the runs will keep coming." Then another wicket falls. "I must not get out now. I must be very careful and pick up the ones I can." Then another wicket falls. "These last two won't last long, I must get them quickly." The head which has stayed down for more than four hours goes up and that is that. A careless shot? An unnecessary shot? A stupid shot? In these situations not many people keep cool and think what is going on in the mind of the man in the batting gloves, although they all apparently know what he should do and are quick to speak when he does "wrong". Only cricket can develop a situation to this stage, leave it in suspense for so long, and then answer it so suddenly.

There was another great moment that day. Lloyd and Kanhai had put on over a hundred for the fourth wicket and England were beginning to look disheartened when D'Oliveira swung one away from Kanhai. He jabbed at it and it went off a thick outside edge to the gully. Cowdrey threw himself to his right and one-handed juggled with the catch. By the time he had made sure of it he was on the ground with his back to the bowler's umpire, and the square-leg umpire was not in the best position to see. Kanhai, who was 85, asked Cowdrey if he had made the catch and when Cowdrey said that he had, Kanhai walked to the pavilion. It was a fine moment and something this match deserved. Those concerned must have been sad when they read in one of the local papers the next day that it was time the umpires were left to umpire matches by themselves. There is surely no substitute for honesty!

So Kanhai departed and the West Indies needed another 129 with six wickets standing to save the follow-on. In the first 75 minutes after lunch Sobers, Holford, Murray and Lloyd followed him, Sobers to a long hop, Holford to a childish run out, and Murray to a full toss. For the Englishmen possibilities had become probabilities. Soon afterwards Griffith swung hopefully at Jones and Parks threw the ball high in the air. One wicket to fall, 12 more runs needed. Two singles and a defiant on-drive by Hall reduced the gap to 6, but then Gibbs stretched forward to Jones and the ball flicked his leg bail. The crowd were stunned. Their heroes were going to follow-on. The England side walked off all smiles and chatter, oblivious of the awesome silence around them.

They had just over seven hours to bowl the West Indies out a second time but as they reached the pavilion, so it began to rain. It rained hard and within twenty minutes the ground was a lake. Following-on in their own country was an unusual experience for the West Indies, but the clouds crept up from the south and wept, in sorrow and support, for it left them with 100 minutes less to bat. Surely England could not bowl them out in just five and a half hours, with the West Indies needing only 205 to make England bat again.

The crowd was much smaller on the last day. They had been disillusioned the day before and were clearly not prepared to consider the possibilities of a West Indies defeat, especially as it would have meant taking another day off to see it. As a result the atmosphere was not now so vibrant and it was going to need an effort from the players to key themselves up for the battle ahead. Previously the crowd had done this for them. But the day got off to the most uneventful start of the five. After three overs it began to look as if the players were already waiting for half-past five. There was a flutter as Nurse was dropped in the gully in D'Oliveira's first over and not much more when, after an hour and a half's play, he misread Titmus's length and was bowled.

Ten minutes before lunch Camacho, playing in his first Test, drove Barrington low and hard into the covers. Graveney, who seemed to grow younger with every hour of this match, jumped to his left at short extra-cover and took a magnificent catch. Graveney takes a catch in much the same way as he makes a stroke: elegantly and with time to spare. He did well to get to this one, but as he threw the ball in the air afterwards it all seemed so easy.

At 100 for 2 with little more than three and a half hours to go the game still seemed to be moving quietly to its now logical conclusion. Another wicket after lunch and England would still have an outside chance, but it was not to be. Kanhai again took root and Butcher gave him solid support. Slowly the score mounted. Runs were as important as time to the West Indies. If they could get past 205 every run counted double as it would mean that England would themselves have to bat again.

An hour after the interval the West Indies were 164 for 2, needing only 41 to make England bat again. But before another run was scored Kanhai stepped out to drive Hobbs without quite getting to the pitch and Hobbs made ground to his left and took a splended return catch. Lloyd came phlegmatically out, played forward to Jones, was caught by Titmus at square short-leg, and walked phlegmatically back again. It was probably now that the West Indian batsmen lost their nerve. With six wickets still to fall there was not the slightest reason to suspect that they were incapable of saving the game. But by now the tension had returned. The crowd had grown a little and they, too, seemed to sense disaster. They had been shouting while things were going well, but now in their anxiety they grew quieter. Every single was cheered to the echo and all eyes turned to the scoreboard as the West Indies came nearer to safety.

Surprisingly Holford, not Sobers, came in next. At once Titmus hit him on the pad and all England appealed, but in vain. Then Jones bowled to Holford with ten men up for the catch. It was brave stuff by Cowdrey but at 178 for 4 the West Indies needed only 27 more. Even when Holford played no shot at a straight ball from Titmus an England victory was no more than a distant hope. But the West Indies were disintegrating under pressure and twelve minutes before tea Cowdrey switched Brown for Jones at the North end of the ground. Brown will never bowl a better over than his second of this spell.

Butcher, who had batted nearly two and a half hours, shuffled across his wicket to the first ball, which nipped back at him off the seam and hit him halfway up the leg. Eleven voices asked and the umpire said yes. Murray got his bat to the next three balls, but went back to the fifth. Keeping a shade low, it hit him where it had hit Butcher. Again the appeal, and again the umpire's finger. The West Indies were now 180 for 7 and before the crowd could grasp what had happened Griffith was making his way ponderously out. He took guard very deliberately and settled over his bat. Brown started in. The ball pitched outside his leg stump, but as Griffith lunged at it, it hit him on the left foot and crashed into his leg stump. The West Indies were 180 for 8, and the Englishmen hardly dared to smile as they came into tea. Victory must be theirs; it was tantalisingly poised just two wickets away, and there were only Hall and Gibbs to come—although Sobers, nought not out, was leaning on his bat in his own angular way at the other end.

Nothing is definite in cricket until it is in the scorebook. Hall played forward four times in Brown's first over after the tea interval and four times Parks took the ball. It went an inch over the off stump and an inch wide of it. Then it missed the outside edge of Hall's bat by half a millimetre and finally it went over the top of the middle stump. All the England fielders were round the bat now. In Brown's next over Hall played forward and the ball flew high off the bat between forward short-leg's hands. As luck would have it the short-leg was Boycott, the only England player in glasses and the only one who never fields close except when, like this, there are ten men round the bat. Hall got a run and when Sobers drove Titmus handsomely over mid-off, the crowd suddenly seemed to sense that the West Indies had a chance. Cowdrey did all he could to keep Sobers away from the strike, but Hall's enormous forward defensive thrust was in working order by now. He played two maidens from Titmus and after each stroke the crowd yelled with delight and Hall looked just as pleased. As island coach he had been teaching the youth of Trinidad how to play forward in practice, and he was delighted to have the chance to show them how it really worked.

After Sobers's four the West Indies needed less than twenty to make England bat again. In an over's time the new ball was due. Should Cowdrey take it? Barrington had just curled one agonisingly past the edge of Hall's bat, but the fast bowlers had had a rest. Cowdrey talked to Titmus, Graveney, and then Barrington, and after the 75th over he took it. And in spite of the Chinese taxi driver he was probably right, but in these situations the only thing that succeeds is success and this Cowdrey did not have. Many people said therefore that he should not have taken the new ball. It was a fine point. Anyway the West Indies saved the match and Cowdrey bowled the last over to Sobers, who politely took only a single from it. As the players came in the spectators invaded the field and swarmed round Sobers and Hall as if they were cheering a two-wicket victory. Some of them were singing calypsos. They had not had much to cheer during the five days and this was their moment. The England side walked in slowly and sadly, only too well aware of what they had missed and wondering if they would have another chance. Cowdrey shook Sobers's hand and smiled, and no wonder. It may have been sad for England and for the West Indies too, but it had been a great triumph for the game of cricket.

4

Tear gas and the dollar

'I had to leave a little girl in Kingston Town', was Belafonte's lament, but it is not a chance to take. Jamaica is one of the most beautiful of the West Indian islands and yet it is one of the most unsatisfactory. It is a country of extreme contrasts, of wealth and poverty, of squalor and beauty and of tourism and local life.

Jamaica is a big island and in three weeks it is impossible to see all of it or to absorb fully the parts one does see. All the same I was in this time able to appreciate the tremendous physical beauty and maybe to understand the taxi driver who on the way to Palisadoes Airport brought out of the glove pocket a heavy automatic pistol and half-turning to me said, "there can be no beatitude ·for criminals". There was no mistaking his tone of voice either and the pistol was loadeď.

Palisadoes Airport balloons off the narrow causeway which links Kingston and the mainland to Port Royal, Morgan's infamous city most of which was destroyed by an earthquake and what is left lingers on like a ghostly skeleton for what it once was. The dark misty peaks of the Blue Mountains overlook the Airport and it is an exciting drive to the mainland past the grotesquely shaped cacti which grow out of the sand and stones at the side of the road. The moment of arriving in any country is exciting and even though the towers of the flour mills and oil storage tanks and several other necessary adjuncts of city life are soon visible they are somehow different.

We turned left at the roundabout where the causeway joins the mainland. To start with the road was poor but now and then there were stretches of dual carriageway which made 60 seem a reasonable speed and not supersonic. Into Kingston and past new factories and office blocks, but now the road was narrower and the bicyclists and pedestrians more difficult to avoid.

Children raced down the pavements while the adult

population moved at a more sleepy pace and all the time there were the angry horns of the metered cabs and occasionally the more sophisticated blare of the big limousines. Alongside a new five-storey block there was a ramshackle two-storey wooden building which housed a "fresh cut" sandwich bar and had a myriad of Coca-Cola, 7-up and orange drink advertisements on the outside. It was new and old and the old seemed to fit in better.

On through the city and the conditions get better and then worse. First there are the houses set back from the road surrounded by trees and the blaze of colour which comes from a tropical garden, the shopping centres are also set back, and it is airy and cheerful. But then after losing my way and going further downtown the streets got narrower, the alleyways darker and more suspicious and the faces on the pavements became more sullen. I passed two Rastafarians with their uncut hair and wild beards and the children are in rags and the smell is not too good. This is downtown Kingston.

But back on the right road again the streets unopen and eventually onto a dual carriageway past the Caymanas club and on towards Spanish Town which has for a long time been the eyesore of Jamaica. It was seven years since I had last been there and the improvement was remarkable. The poverty was not now so stark and obvious. The wooden shacks were better cared for and it was more than just bare existence. The people are still very poor but there was more in life for them than there used to be.

Kingston to Montego Bay is signposted as 109 miles. The road goes across the island to Ocho Rios and then on another 60 miles up the North Coast to "Mo Bay". There are other ways, but this is the shortest and it is spectacular too. At first it is a relief to be out of Spanish Town and the road winds through a narrow valley with a river first on the right and then after crossing a bridge which has no parapets, on the left. It is beautiful in contrast to the urban life, but not really Jamaica yet. For a time the country flattens out with the rich tropical vegetation of trees and flowers and bushes. There are banana trees, palm trees, bougainvillea, poinsettia, hibiscus and the hills in front. After a time the road begins to wind on and up in a series of never-ending curves. As the car struggles on in second gear exciting new panoramic views open up. Looking down into the valley and up on the other side there is every conceivable shade of green from the light greeny-yellow of the burnt grass land to the deep green of the heavily wooded slopes across the valley.

The road is narrow and occasionally a horn blares furiously and with tyres squeaking the two cars pass, just. And then in front maybe, there is an old and heavy lorry struggling up in first gear. Overtaking is impossible and the clouds of black smoke which pour out of the exhaust are not the pleasantest of travelling companions. For a mile or more the procession goes on and finally driven to despair it is overtaken round yet another bend.

Round the next bend there are two men walking slowly upwards and then two bends later, and this is one of the sharpest, there are some women selling bananas to any who stop. The bananas would be good but the bend is such that stopping is impossible. Then a few hundred yards further on there is a group of huts on the outside of the road. One of them, which looks like an outsize bus stop, is blazoned with the usual advertisements Coca-Cola, 7-up, etc. and is a small shop selling rum, drinks, cigarettes, fruit and many other similar things. Beside it, there will be a small road running down the hill and it is possible to catch a glimpse of the roofs of the shacks which make up a little village.

There are usually a number of people standing around the shop and whenever a car comes by they stop talking and stare. Even the children playing in the dust break off and look. These little villages are left behind in a cloud of dust in about five seconds.

About six or seven miles before Ocho Rios the road begins to drop. Then suddenly the light goes and the temperature drops as the car plunges into a deep channel of rock. The road winds through the sharply descending gorge and on each side the rocky walls which are three parts covered with tropical ferns rise high above the car. There are trees growing on top of the rock and down below the shade is complete. The drop gets steeper and the road more bendy and it seems the descent is never going to end. But after ten minutes the car suddenly rounds another corner and is swamped by sunlight. This is Fern Gully and it is an awe-inspiring ten minutes. It is the journey from one world into another and this now is Ocho Rios, the North Coast and tourism.

Jamaica has three main industries which are sugar, bauxite and tourism. The North Coast takes care of the tourism and with twelve expensive hotels Ocho Rios is second only to Montego Bay. Tourism is profitable and necessary for Jamaica, but in some ways it has had a bad effect on the island. It is no way from the United States and the exchange rates make it a cheap holiday for the Americans and Jamaica needs the dollars. As a result a large part of the island is geared simply to extract as many dollars in as short a time as possible from the Americans. The unsatisfactory part about it is that it produces something which is not really Jamaica and a phoney section of people few of whom are Jamaicans doing all they can to sell the island without caring too much for it.

The contrast between the North Coast and the South is extreme. In a rum shop in Kingston I asked a man if he had ever been to Montego Bay and he looked at me and intoned, "Montego Bay" almost as if I had mentioned the Philippines. For him Montego Bay was unattainable. The atmosphere of the North Coast is created by hotels for which US $60 is not an expensive price for bed, breakfast and dinner, while the taxi driver and his gun are more in keeping with the Kingston docks and Spanish Town.

The second night I was in Montego Bay the manager of my hotel asked me if I would like to go with him and his assistant manager to a night club called the Cats Corner. As I walked through the door into the dark smokey atmosphere Engelbert Humperdinck and 'The Last Waltz' were blaring out of the juke box. I had a couple of drinks and then left the other four—they had brought two girls with them—and went to the bar to buy another round. The bar was crowded and after a ten minute wait I pushed through to the counter when a female West Indian voice made me an offer. I looked to my left to see an attractive coloured girl in a dark green dress. I declined, but she went on talking in a pleasant lilting voice tinged with a trace of American and flashing her shiny eyes around the room as she talked.

She told me she came from Kingston and I asked her how.

Momentarily she looked at the ceiling and then back.

"I never thought I would get here," she said.

She was one of the youngest of a family of twelve children and they lived in the rough part of Kingston. Her father was always out of work, but when she was fourteen she got a job as a "secretary" in an office (which probably meant a tea girl) and the "few shillings" she earned made life more bearable. On her way to work each day she passed near the docks and the sailors used to whistle at her and she realised that she had an attractive body and before long for a dollar or two she used to "go" with them and by her standards she was rich.

I asked her again how she made the breakthrough to Montego Bay. Once more her eyes lit up. She had had a marvellous month when every man she met gave her about ten times what she asked and in a short time she had saved the money to buy the clothes which were necessary for Montego Bay and to rent the apartment she would need. She had had elocution lessons and she certainly talked more slowly and audibly than many Jamaicans. Montego Bay was to her a paradise she had for a long time had no hope or thought of reaching. Now she was there and charging US $25 a time. When she finished she looked up at me:

"You know, I never dreamt I would get here." She was happy.

I returned with the drinks to the others and was amused to see that within ten minutes she was dancing attentively with a fifty year old amply proportioned American who needed no urging. This story shows the contrasts of the two halves of the country as they are and also as they appear in the minds of many of the people who live there. Kingston and Montego Bay are 109 miles apart, but in ways they are many worlds apart and this cannot be good for a small island to have such dramatic differences so near to each other.

The beaches in Ocho Rios are marvellous and although there are big hotels and all the trimmings to make life easy for the tourists, it retains a lot of the charm of a small fishing village. A Jamaica Inn special, white rum, pale rum, Tia Maria, Pernod, orange and pineapple juice, is a good halfway drink. It has rather a strange taste and it took me half a glass to make up my mind if I liked it. The Pernod gives it the

slimy feeling of drinking a beaten egg, but by the end of one
I was quite prepared to have another. Pernod is an unlikely
drink to find in Jamaica, but then so was the table d'hote
menu which boasted escargots followed by roast beef and
Yorkshire pudding a little out of place.

The road improves going on up the coast from Ocho Rios
and the country is flatter, the land more fertile and the
farming is better organised and on a bigger scale. The scenery
is still beautiful too and soon after leaving Ocho Rios the
road crosses Dunns River Falls which are featured in colour
in every book and brochure which has been written about
Jamaica and usually with attractive girls lying in unlikely
poses alongside. The waterfall is small but it is a scene of
complete serenity. The water comes gently almost apologetically down the hillside through the rich foliage before
disappearing into the sea.

But Jamaica even here is full of strange contrasts and a few
hundred yards further on there is the bauxite factory, large
and red with the pipes crossing over the road to the pier
where the ships are loaded. The countryside around is
covered with the red dust of the bauxite. The factory and
Dunns River Falls are two of Jamaica's greatest assets, but
nature must have put them alongside each other with a wry
smile on her face.

The towns and villages are now vastly less primitive than
those in the mountains before Ocho Rios. The big cars
bringing passengers from Montego Bay Airport do not look
so incongruous. The road passes one big hotel after another,
the Hilton, Discovery Bay, Runaway Bay; all marvellous in
their way and at their own price. Runaway Bay is on its own
with something like 2,500 acres, and it has its own golf
course and every other conceivable amenity all of which are
expertly supervised by Fred Perry, three times winner at
Wimbledon in the thirties and with a figure which would be a
credit to any present day champion.

From Ocho Rios on, all prices are quoted in $ US and if a
waiter is tipped in sterling, which is still the official Jamaican
currency, he looks first at it and then at you. I was sure too
in Montego Bay that when taxi drivers realised they were
going to be paid in pounds and not dollars, and it's a very
short ride for less than a pound, they added a bit on.

And so to "Mo Bay". It was dark when I arrived, but lighted signs revealed that the hotels started twelve miles outside the town. They were all in the most magnificent settings. They stood at the end of palm tree avenues and they all had wonderful beaches and a swimming pool somewhere around. Mine was among them and for five days I listened to the American accent—mostly the drawling Southern type, in hotels, on the beaches, on the golf course, in the restaurants and in the night clubs. Everyone wore tartan Bermuda shorts and said, "Why, we don't pay $3.20 for that back home", at the same time. Local life was entirely subjective to the dollar. The Jamaicans were hidden behind bars, in buses, behind the counters in the shops and when I picked up my telephone after a long wait a deep sexy Jamaican voice said, "Operator".

Montego Bay has a wonderful climate in January and it is an attractive town. It is overlooked by some hills on the far side of the bay and coming in from Ocho Rios there is pleasant open country and a golf course with electric caddies racing over it. There is also Rose Hall, the old plantation Great House where Annie Palmer, the White Witch of Rose Hall, lived. She was a beautiful and cruel woman who is reputed to have murdered three husbands and many slaves and lovers before she was finally killed by her slaves in 1831. I spent one afternoon looking down on Montego Bay from William Hill's magnificent house high in the hills on the far side of the bay and it was an unforgettable picture. That day there was an American aircraft carrier in the harbour. The steely grey of the hull and the rows of gleaming aircraft on deck were more colours to add to an already unbelievable range. There were the flowers, the bouganvillea, the hibiscus, the reds, the pinks, the yellows, the purples around the swimming pool and then the different greens as the hill sloped away below us to the fields and then to the roofs of the town. On the far side the country opened up again with all its different colours and then there was the blue sky and the translucent almost green water in the harbour. Every hour or so a quiet drone from the north would announce the arrival of another aeroplane and it would come planing in like some great silver bird over the sea. The airport is by the sea and so when the aircraft crossed the coast they were almost

down and these machines would glide in over the water the
other side of the aircraft carrier, looking from where we
were so small and so slow. The only other view in the West
Indies I saw to compare with this was from the Governor's
House in St. Lucia looking out over a much smaller harbour
in which at the time *The France* was anchored.

This all seems a long way from cricket and it is somehow
wrong that an island as beautiful, and this was only a very
small part of it, can produce a crowd of people who angrily
throw bottles at a Test Match which is not going their way
and have themselves to be checked with tear gas. But
Kingston and Montego Bay might be a thousand, not just 109
miles apart.

There are so many places to go and almost everything that
is scenically possible has been crammed into Jamaica. The
other road to the North Coast winds through the Blue
Mountains and emerges south of Ocho Rios between Port
Antonio and Port Maria. The heavily wooded slopes, the
water courses in the valleys, the exciting shapes of the rocks,
the terrifying sharpness of the bends in the road and of
course the myriad of colours made it a thrilling journey. I
spent most of the time looking out of the rear window as I
could hardly bear to let the views go.

The Blue Mountains produce the finest coffee in the world
and one of the great joys of Jamaica is breakfast and
unlimited coffee. As well as the coffee plantations there are
the banana plantations and the orange groves and other
citrus fruit. There is something wonderfully satisfying about
driving alongside an orange grove with the fruit hanging
under the dark green leaves. In England, oranges seem to have
for ever lain in boxes or baskets in greengrocers' shops, almost
as if they were made and not grown and it is just as exciting
to see the green bunches of bananas hanging on from each
banana tree attached to the tree by a thick umbilical cord.

The North Coast is beautiful too. The beaches are ideal,
the sand near-white, the water pale green and transparent and
the reefs far enough out not to make bathing difficult and
near enough in to look down on them through a
glass-bottomed boat.

Port Antonio offers the most expensive hotel in the world

and a fascinating journey on a raft down the Rio Grande seeing the river and then taking on the rapids. It was at Port Antonio that Captain Bligh of the Bounty landed in 1793. Another fine sight is the Blue Hole, a lagoon with its deep, blue water surrounded by the rich tropical vegetation.

The banana port of Oracabessa is a charming little town. Seven years ago I went to Oracabessa early in the morning and listened to men who had been loading the bananas onto the ship all night singing 'Day-O'. They were scantily clad and glistening with sweat and the song was almost inaudible, yet the mournful and strangely tuneful sound was unforgettably beautiful.

Each town or village on the North Coast has its own attractions, either physical or man-made. It is an easy world to live in as long as there is enough money to pay the bills. There are Planter's Punches all day, and at night, calypsos, the flaming limbo and fire eaters. The calypso in Jamaica is different to the sharper more clipped Trinidadian calypso. Sung the Jamaican way calypso is more tuneful and less rhythmical.

In Georgetown towards the end of the tour I talked to The Mighty Sparrow about this difference. His chief musician Vasso de Freitas who was with him described the Jamaican calypso as a mentor. I had not heard of a mentor and Sparrow quickly came to my rescue, "Jamaican calypso is like Trinidad calypso used to be before it developed. It is old fashioned, but I hope that the calypso I sing will become universal." The difference is easy to spot if, say, 'Jamaica Farewell' played in Jamaica is compared with 'Mister Walker', in Trinidad.

Jamaica being a tourist island obviously cashes in on calypso and although it is different from Trinidad it is still fun to listen to. One night in Montego Bay two singers arrived behind my chair after dinner and started to play their guitars and sing. 'The Big Bamboo' came first, then 'The Watermelon', 'The Mermaid' and a few more. The words and the emphasis they were given might have shocked the Lord Chamberlain, but they were very funny and there is something about the West Indian voice which seems to take the harshest interpretation away from them.

Music and song in Jamaica is both local and cosmopolitan. At the Cats Corner a juke box blared and Engelbert Humperdinck cleared his voice so that the 'Last Waltz' followed 'Yellow Bird' without a moment's pause. Before lunch at the Colony Hotel the uniformed police band gave a delightful display of wind and brass round the swimming pool. They were good, but somehow it was surprising even for the benefit of tourists to hear tunes better suited to a ceremonial march down Whitehall.

At the Sheraton Hotel which was the liveliest in Kingston, the calypso band is manned by an Australian group. They maintained a high standard, but again it was curious to see a lot of Jamaicans getting wound up to 'Come back Liza' which was coming out of Australian mouths. Then on another evening at the Sheraton a Jamaican gave a splendid crooning impersonation of Bing Crosby.

But Jamaica has its own dance, 'the Rock Steady'. It is a variation of the calypso dance and is a quieter edition of 'Ska', its predecessor. The guide book I found in my hotel bedroom was very definite. "Sensuous and throbbing. The Rock-Steady beat has completely dominated the dance loving people of Jamaica, having them turn out in droves nightly to surrender their bodies to this new Jamaican rhythm."

It then instructs how to dance the 'Rock Steady'. "Just relax the whole body and allow the pulsating Rock-Steady rhythms to 'seep' into your system. Then 'under the spell' you sway your limp arms and shoulders from side to side accompanied by a one foot shuffle going in any direction. Occasionally you may stand in one place and raise your shoulders alternately to the beat. Forget partners—just relax and let your 'oily' bodies sway in and out and go with the Rock-Steady beat." Or do as you please.

This rather oversold it although it would have been excellent advice for anyone going out to bat on the remarkable Sabina Park wicket in the Second Test. But it was fun to dance and easy to do as long as you were relaxed, moved freely and moved in rhythm.

But why on Monday February 12th at 2.33 p.m. when the West Indies were 204 for 5 did the bottles come and continue with such hostility that the Riot Squad had to use tear gas to restore order? It would take a lot longer than two weeks to discover all there is to know about Kingston, but talking and looking and listening I got some idea. Kingston has a lot of mysteries, several undesirable sides and a number of complexes in its midst.

I got my first impression of the people there on the night I arrived back from Montego Bay where MCC had continued their maddeningly perverse habit of doing badly when it did not matter and had followed on against the Jamaica Colts. Throughout the Caribbean the service in hotels and restaurants was very slow. Waiting to order dinner and then to eat it was rather like catching a glimpse of eternity. Yet in the end it arrived; the waiters grinned innocently unconscious maybe of the time and if I wanted to be angry I was quickly disarmed and almost invariably got involved in a discussion about cricket. "Man, you see Sobers today?" and on it would go. It did not matter that the soup was tepid.

I had been forewarned that in the West Indies there were only two speeds: dead slow and stop. That first evening in Kingston it was dead-stop. Nothing happened and I began to get anxious. When at last a waiter appeared I suggested that something should be happening soon, but instead of smiling and giving the most plausible of excuses be stared nervously at the wall beside me occasionally looking at me out of the side of his eye. He never looked me in the face.

The captain—American terminology in hotels is baffling—who apparently comes after the Maitre D, was a small man with a moustache and a rather severe face and another time I was irritated after half an hour's wait at breakfast, I was fairly abrupt. The captain was upset and later told the Maitre D who was Swiss that I only talked to him in the way I did because he was black and I was white. All round the West Indies the problem of colour was always present, but this was the only time it showed itself in this way. It was insecurity by the Jamaicans, because as soon as I grinned or laughed or showed them that I was human and friendly, they were delightful people. At first some of them seemed instinctively suspicious.

Kingston is a sprawling urban conglomeration with its poor parts and its rich parts. Much of Jamaica is poor and life in the inland villages particularly is very simple. When people have the opportunity or the desire to better themselves their

first and quite natural desire is to make for the "big city".
And so to Kingston they go, but their problems then begin.
The education is bad in Kingston for those who cannot
afford it; there is a high rate of unemployment and there is a
large dock area which as in any other country attracts crime.
It is difficult therefore for a poor person coming to live in
Kingston to get a start. If he does not, crime may provide the
answer.

The Rastafarians are another bad influence. They are
a sect who believe that Haile Selassie the Emperor of
Ethiopia is God and that Ethiopia is heaven and all they want
is to go there. They are easily distinguishable by their long
unkempt beards and are mostly unemployed as they are a
bad influence on society. They are all the time trying to
increase their numbers and so continual recruitment goes on.
If a person refuses to have anything to do with their
movement as soon as he is approached he is alright, but if he
shows an initial interest and then wants to back out he is in
trouble and qualifies for anything including murder. The
Rastafarians are an entirely unprincipled set of people who
are responsible for a big percentage of the crime in Kingston.

Another evil influence is Obeahism, the Jamaican form of
Voodoo. To practise Obeahism is an offence which is
punishable by imprisonment, but I was assured by a Jamaican
in a rum shop not far from my hotel that it is still practised.
The Obeah man is supposed to control good and evil spirits
which he imparts to believers at secret nocturnal sessions. I
was unable to discover more than just the bare details and
when I asked this man about it he said uncertainly that it still
existed, but he shut up the moment I tried to press him for
something more specific. It may have been strange for him to
find an Englishman in the rum shop and whether my being
there and talking to him may have had sinister implications
or simply that the very mention of Voodoo frightened him I
did not discover. Anyway, I bought him some rum and we
parted friends.

Add to all this the fact that the Africans are a volatile
excitable people whose emotions run high for the smallest
reason and also that there is a continual feud between the
Africans and the small, shrewd Chinese community and that
a Chinese umpire gave Butcher out the ball before the first

bottle was thrown, and the riots became almost predictable; and so did the taxi driver's gun.

It was extremely hot. The ground was full and maybe overfull as West Indian spectators have a way of squeezing in; a certain amount of rum had been drunk and as in all West Indian crowds some betting was bound to have been going on. And with the West Indies doing so badly there was a deep sense of disappointment which can so easily and quickly turn to resentment. All that was needed was the first bottle and 2.33 that afternoon it came.

Somehow Kingston and the Second Test belonged to each other. Rioters, bottles, tear gas, a terrible wicket, a century by Cowdrey, a remarkable all-round performance by Sobers, an unscheduled sixth day and a dramatic finish were the essential ingredients of the match. It was a match which, but for the riots, England must have won and it became a match which they were lucky not to lose.

There is a similarity between the setting at Sabina Park and that at Queen's Park Oval. The Blue Mountains on the North side, taller and more distantly forbidding than the range in Trinidad, but hazy and mysteriously capped with cloud are perhaps more impressive, but less beautiful. The large green Pavilion at square-leg is a handsome structure and from its top balcony the sea on either side of the causeway leading out to Palisadoes and Port Royal glistens in the sun.

Yet in spite of the sea and the mountains the ground itself is small and unattractively urban. The tall metal pylons holding the football floodlights at each corner of the ground do not help. The stands, except for those next to the Pavilion are cramped and old, the popular East side is just empty ground with the bare branches of half-a-dozen lignum vitae providing the only stand accommodation. In the South-East corner there is an ugly mound of terracing which was to become so infamous. Most of the stands could have done with a coat of paint and the lignum vitae were in need of some new or at any rate some more branches. There was a certain amount of branch space in the trees at the North end and the floodlight pylons were also popular vantage points. On the first day of the Test, Shell were giving away vivid orange paper sun hats and the crowds packed tightly into the stands looked like serried ranks of school children. There was also the occasional orange hat poking out from the green foliage at the top of the palm trees.

Sabina Park is the smallest Test ground in the world and when Hall went back to the end of his run he was no more than five yards from where we were sitting in the Press box beside the sightscreen at the South end. To prevent the Press box becoming oppressively hot, air conditioning and windows have been installed. It was comfortable for us, but curious for the crowd, for in mid-afternoon when they were sweltering they could see English journalists in the Press box pulling on sweaters to protect themselves against the air conditioning which must, I suppose, have seemed to them to be just another variation of Mad Dogs and Englishmen. The only drawback was to feel the atmosphere. The box was at ground level and it was like watching through a periscope.

The dramas of the match began some time before as the wicket had been relaid and it had not had time to settle down and no one was sure how it was going to behave. Before the start of the match wide cracks had already appeared as the moisture dried and it lay shining like a vast cracked mirror. In hot countries wickets often look like this and are alright as long as the edges of the cracks do not crumble. The 13,000 spectators who gathered in this jumble of a ground to watch England start their innings after Cowdrey had won the toss were in a high ferment of excitement. Excitement at Sabina Park was even more urgent and frenetic than on any other West Indian ground, even Georgetown.

The crowd went through every emotion as England passed 200 for 2 with Cowdrey making 100 before they collapsed to 376 all out. But by then the advantages of batting first were all too obvious. The cracks were now more than half an inch wide and the ball was flying and shooting. The West Indies could make little of it and Snow bowling fast and with excellent length and direction took 7 for 49. The crowd were reduced to near silence as shock followed on shock. The worst they had to endure came when they were expecting relief. At 80 for 4 Sobers came slowly out to tremendous applause, took guard, looked around the field, settled over his bat, was hit on the boot by a shooter and walked slowly back when the umpire confirmed the inevitable.

The West Indies followed-on and although they were given

a fine start by Nurse who played one of the most memorable innings of the tour, wickets kept on falling. Nurse played a ball into his stumps, Camacho received his second straight shooter of the match, Kanhai hooked into square-leg's hands and, one run after lunch, Lloyd received another straight shooter. There was then an agonising and fatal moment for England. Sobers when 3 snicked Brown past Graveney at second slip for four and Graveney in trying to stop it split a finger nail and went off. D'Oliveira took his place at second slip. Sobers played back to the next ball and it flew quite gently off the edge to D'Oliveira who dropped the catch. Three balls later Graveney who only missed one catch on the tour was back in his position. If that catch had been held nothing short of an earthquake would have stopped England winning the match.

Then Butcher played his fateful leg glance at D'Oliveira and was rightly given out caught behind the wicket. Seventy-five minutes playing time were lost and a sixth day of seventy-five minutes was arranged, but after the riots the tension went out of the cricket. The next day, the fifth, Sobers reached a hundred which D'Oliveira clapped rather sadly and then declared leaving England to score 159 in 155 minutes. Sobers himself sent back Boycott and Cowdrey in the first over and when bad light stopped play forty minutes early that night England were 19 for 4 and at the end of the seventy-five agonising minutes the next day had limped to 61 for 8 and safety.

Kingston has its problems of unemployment, poverty and racial dislikes as well as the unhealthy influences of Obeahism and the Rastafarians. Each of these may have contributed in some way to the eruption when it came; each one working on immature temperaments which may well have been already softened by a good deal of rum. It was a combustible mixture. Of course Kingston is not all poverty, crime and riots and in the normal way these may not make themselves felt. I met a vast number of charming and delightful people who could not have entertained me more splendidly and been more charming, but nevertheless Kingston does not have a happy atmosphere.

The feel and atmosphere of a city or a country is not set

by the people, however nice, who entertain one so splendidly. Nor is it set by the cosmopolitan hotels and night clubs and the people who go there. In every city it is the majority and in Kingston it is a poverty-stricken majority who by their attitude to their fellows and their reaction to life give the place its feel. In Kingston there is enough for them to be afraid of.

Kingston did however provide me with one of my greatest pleasures in the West Indies. The Blue Mountain Inn is in the most perfect setting over 1,000 feet up in the Blue Mountains with a small river, the *Mammee*, flowing through the valley below. The house itself was built in 1754 as the Great House of a coffee plantation and it was by some way the best restaurant I went to in nearly three and a half months in the Caribbean. The banana flambé which was cooked with meticulous care beside me was one of the most perfect dishes I have eaten in my life. The restaurant is not cheap, but it is worth every penny piece.

It was an evening too which ended on a delightfully inconsequential West Indian note. I ordered a taxi from inside the restaurant and went into the courtyard to wait for it. There was a Jamaican on duty there and he came up and asked me if I wanted a taxi. I told him that I had already ordered one and he looked at me and then he said,

"So you phoned for one before you came out? Oh yes, sir. Very nice sir."

For all their faults this remark, I think, showed that Kingston and Jamaica are very much a part of the West Indies.

5

An island of tradition

The forty-five minute drive from Seawell Airport through Bridgetown to the West Coast is like looking at a quickfire advertisement for the West Indies. The palm trees, the sugar cane, the poincettia, the old colonial city which has a main street called Broad Street, its own Hilton Hotel, and a bay which is everyone's idea of the tropics with a flotilla of little boats and maybe a big liner at anchor. Then there is the Careenage and Trafalgar Square which combine the beauty and the actuality of history, the rum shops and the wooden shacks flanked incongruously by large garish advertisements. And on to the smart West Coast hotels and their perfect white beaches where the hardest job of the day is rolling over from one side to the other to take another Planter's Punch from the waiter.

Barbados is a holiday island. The West Coast has one of the most ideal coastlines in the West Indies and it has been developed to provide Barbados with a major industry. When tourism becomes important to a country the character of that country can quickly change as the gloss rubs off, but over the years Barbados has successfully resisted change and it has managed to keep its individual character in spite of tourism.

It is the only West Indian island which has never changed hands from the time the English first arrived in 1625 until Independence. There are therefore no French or Spanish or Portuguese or Far Eastern influences in the island and it is peopled by two races. There are the white Bajans who mostly descend from the English colonists and are a small minority, and the black Bajans the descendants of the slaves. These two races evolved a working arrangement after Emancipation and even the recently granted independence has done little to change the basic theme of life.

Sugar is the island's main industry and although colonialism has gone, the ways of the old plantocracy still exist. There are all-white clubs on the island and one gets the impression that things still go on much as they always have done. Life in the island is as one-paced as it is in most agricultural communities in the world. The Bajans go on planting and cutting and grinding sugar cane just as they have always done because it is their life and there is no other way of doing it. It is all that they have known and they are content with it.

Nothing moves very fast and the sleepy reflective atmosphere is undisturbed. The people are delightful, but it requires patience to get to know them. They do not make up their minds quickly and they have an innate reserve although they are by nature friendly. The maid who cleaned my room at the Marine Hotel was always ready to talk to me, but it was not until I had been there a week that she made up her mind about me and began to tell me things without my having to ask. What had made her decide I have no idea, but there was suddenly a noticeable change. I had served my apprenticeship. They also have a strong sense of pride. I was staying with some friends in the island when one morning before breakfast it was discovered that there was no gas. The gas supply came from two cylinders stored outside the house and when one cylinder was empty the cook changed over to the other cylinder and should have reported that the first was empty. She had forgotten to do this and in the fuss that followed she realised that she had been stupid so she put on her hat and went home where she would have stayed in shame if my host had not gone and collected her.

Beyond the perimeter of Seawell Airport the road narrows and, in January and February, the sugar cane rises high on each side until Bridgetown. The canes were ready for cutting, but there was a strike by the sugar harvesters who wanted more money. The unions had prevented the harvest from starting and the employers had refused to pay more. Every day there were reports of impassioned speeches in the papers. When I returned to Barbados in February the strike was still in progress but the people were by then less enthusiastic. At one meeting in St. James which could he heard half a mile away, Mr. Walcott, the leader of the union was speaking, but he received a poor reception.

"He alright, his belly full," was the feeling.

The road winds round a double bend into Bridgetown, goes past the Pepperpot, an open air night club, and through streets with plenty of comfortable villas set back from the road behind small gardens filled with tropical flowers. There are also a number of hotels which now compare rather sadly with their luxurious counterparts on the West Coast. But before the West Coast was developed they were the hotels of Barbados. Most of them are old colonial buildings which flourished in the days when Bridgetown was twenty days sailing from Plymouth. In some of them nothing has changed, in others roof restaurants and barbers' shops and gift shops have sprung up.

On, past this crop of hotels the streets get even narrower and some of them are one way, but no one pays much attention to this. There is a chemist's shop which extravagantly advertises laxatives. At the top of a slight hill the Bridgetown race course opens out on the right and on the left there are the old red brick barracks which have been turned into flats. They are as solidly forbidding as any drill hall of the same date in an English provincial city. The road descends past the barracks and curves round to the right and in a moment the sea glitters through the palm trees which are now set out on either side of the road as if by some landscape gardener.

The bay which opens up on the near side is like an exquisite mirror which is not only beautiful in its own right, but it seems to improve the images it reflects. The sky, the coastline, the small boats and, in the evening, the sun are all faithfully reflected and yet coming out of the water in that setting they seem even better than they are. When the big cruise ships put into Bridgetown they anchor in the bay and their lifeline, a succession of launches chugging to and from the landing stage, ruffle the calm of the water, but they and their parent ship add to the fascination and excitement of the scene. The bay was to be seen at its most beautiful in the evening. Every day coming back from the cricket I would pass it with the sun almost in the sea. At this time of day with the red ball of the sun staring out of the sky and its reflection out of the water the colours were different. Near too, the water was black and steely and the further west I looked it became first a gentle orange before finally bursting into flame at the horizon. The boats in the bay were sharply and colourfully etched in this setting and it was a scene of overwhelming tranquillity. Some evenings I stopped to watch the sun go down beyond the horizon. In the tropics it goes fast and at the moment it disappears there is a brilliant green flash and then the twilight is there exactly as if the stage lights have been turned off.

From this reflective scene the road becomes a street with shops and cinemas and small dingy restaurants on either side. It presents a typical picture of the urban West Indies. The cars soon slow down almost to a halt as a horse and cart moves slowly down the middle of the road chased by a fanfare of horns, but utterly unmoved. The pavements are crowded and there are women walking upright and confident with loads piled high on their heads. Their hands swing casually at their sides and the loads never fall off. There are small groups of men standing on the pavement talking and laughing—laughter plays a big part in West Indian life. There is plenty of movement and bustle, but little purposeful urgency. If you stop and ask a Barbadian a question he will say nothing for a moment. Then he will probably rub his chin, "Oh yes, let me see now," will be the rather unpromising start. But then uncertainly at first and with plenty of corrections thrown in the answer will come, but not before you feel that your direct question demanding a direct answer has thrown him out of his stride.

At the end of this street in the middle of Bridgetown is the Careenage which is the old inner port and it is pure Treasure Island. This small narrow piece of water leads off the main bay like an arrow head. The schooners with their masts and rigging etched against the sky like so many trees in winter, still tie up alongside the warves. There were always plenty of small children playing on the parapets of the bridge. When someone threw a coin into the water several of them dived off the bridge to retrieve it. Then they swam laughing and shouting to the side of the schooners with one child holding up his glittering prize. But apart from these children there was never any movement in the Careenage. The ships lay motionless and apparently unattended except maybe for a sailor smoking in the sun on deck. There was no movement on shore either and obviously loading and unloading went on early in the morning. The schooners are sturdy weather-beaten ships which have sailed around the islands for many years. The Careenage was like this when Long John Silver stumped his way through the Caribbean, but it is a scene which has not been consciously preserved. It is just there as it always has been.

The bridge over the Careenage is near the head of the arrow and driving over it the way of life of the sea continues on either side, untouched by modern times. But over the bridge the mass of parked and moving cars and the shouts of taxi drivers trying to attract tourists and the tourists themselves wearing extravagant straw hats with every kind of camera slung over their shoulders are a stark reminder of the present. This is Trafalgar Square. Over the bridge to left is the statue of Nelson; older and shorter but just as erect as in London.

Looking over the bridge into Trafalgar Square and above the frenzied cars and the impatient tourists, the solid, stone nineteenth century House of Assembly stands impressively behind a thin veil of green foliage from the trees around it and beside it is a similar building which is the G.P.O. The whole scene is a fascinating mixture of old and new. The Careenage offers endless possibilities for there is always something new to see whether it is in the water, on the schooners, up by the warehouses or in the faces of the throng leaning over the parapets or walking slowly along the pavement in Trafalgar Square. But the best time to see and appreciate the beauty of the Careenage and Trafalgar Square is as night is falling or in the early morning when there are not so many visible and distracting signs of twentieth century commercialism. The beautiful colouring of a tropical sunrise or sunset makes a glorious background, but it is an exciting scene at any time of the day. The slow time-no-object walk of the Bajans on the bridge fit in with the setting. The scampering feet and excited screams of the children lend it an immediacy and the handsome schooners give it a reflective glory.

Nelson stands looking down Broad Street with its banks and camera shops and big stores as well as the street vendors. He is more and more submerged by the buildings, but is photographed unceasingly, children try and touch his feet and the American accent which would have sounded strange to his ears rings out. But even Horatio Nelson would have been unable to fight off a modern day tourist invasion.

The journey through Bridgetown continues first in a one-way system which leads back into Broad Street about two hundred yards up the road from Nelson. The smartness and gloss of the immediate neighbourhood of Trafalgar Square soon vanishes. The shops are smaller with paint flaking off the doors and windows, there are more street sellers, there are women on the pavements with their own shopping piled high on their heads and there are the rum shops. It is back to the urban West Indies. In three minutes the car is out of Georgetown with open ground on the right of the road and the sea on the left. Here, it always seems to be windy and the palm trees wave about with their clutches of green coconuts just under the fronds looking like so many gnarled pumpkins. On the right comes a small bevy of gift shops and boutiques and a restaurant all known as Pelican Village, where the prices are high, but the prawn cocktail good.

The road passes close to Kensington Oval and then at the traffic lights which are by the market, just after Worrell's Meat Depot and the largest of the signs saying, "Drink Pepsi Cola The Big One", turns left. There are always people at this crossroads. The market was usually busy and so were the other small shops including of course the rum shops, but it was a meeting place too. There were always groups of Bajans, some talking, some standing. These crossroads were in the middle of a large group of poor houses and they too were similar to those on other islands. They are raised off the ground and are built out of wood, but they look frail enough to be flattened by the first gust of wind. Wherever I went in Barbados I was surprised to find that these houses with their obvious signs of poverty were kept quite beautifully. They may not be attractive but they are tidy inside and out. The West Indian women as they walk down the street with a load on their heads have a proud and dignified bearing and they use the slender resources they have to give their houses the same look. Driving through the small roads in-between the houses the scene was always the same. There were masses of children playing about and every now and then a mother would stand on the small steps leading up to the door and scold one of them in a furious voice. The child that had been chastised would sometimes penitently, sometimes rebelliously approach the steps while the others would continue playing. It was an international scene in a different setting.

I found the day to day life of the people in the island more relaxed than anywhere else. There were usually people crossing the road on foot at these traffic lights. At first I blew my horn furiously, but it did no good. They would turn and look at me and smile and continue across at the same pace and as I drove past they would wave at me. It was at these traffic lights when I was coming into Bridgetown one morning that an elderly Bajan on a bicycle who had also stopped for the red light, looked through the window of my taxi and asked me how I was and if I was happy. He listened carefully when I assured him that I was very happy and then he grinned with childish delight.

Just over the lights is a smart undertaker's shop. It is strategically placed too because by rights there should, just outside, be one bad accident an hour. Opposite the undertaker's and rather incongruously placed was another rum shop and while I was in the island it appeared to do the better business.

The road now leads to the West Coast, but it is still as bumpy and as narrow. There are deep open drains at the side of the tarmac which make passing an oncoming lorry or bus an interesting experience. Another hazard is the pedestrians for the people like nothing better in the West Indies than to get together at the roadside by the shops and they stand well out into the road. After seven or eight minutes dodging the drains and sending pedestrians flying into the shops it is a surprise to come on the large supermarket at Carlton. It is just like any other supermarket and it was worth knowing because a gallon bottle of rum costs next to nothing. If it had been a little cooler and the sun not so bright outside, it might have been any supermarket in which I have ever been. Soon after Carlton the road curves round to the left and there is a sign indicating the drive of the Paradise Beach Club which is the first of the big hotels.

The next ten miles present a continual vista of luxury. There are hotels and restaurants, a nine-hole golf course, private houses, some on the golf course, some looking onto the sea with their own private stretch of beach and there are the extensive amenities of the hotels, water skiing, glass-bottomed boats, dancing, steel bands, calypso singers, limbo dancers and fire eaters. All are ideal and it is a stimulating form of luxury. And the best of all the luxuries is the cold buffet lunch which the hotels serve in turn on different days through the week. There are plates of freshly cooked lobsters and prawns, every kind of salad imaginable, plates of chicken done in several different ways, plenty of red underdone Texan beef and lots of exciting things which taste delicious and have incomprehensible names. Then there are fresh pineapples, bananas, mangos, grapefruit and all the tropical fruits. It is wonderful too to go to bed and listen to the sea gently lapping the sand and the continuous rustle of the palm trees in the wind. These hotels have different bands playing each night and once a week they have a floor show. The dance-floors are outside and in the Paradise Beach Club the bar is ten paces one way, the sea ten paces the other and the dining room is no further off. All perfect.

Barbados is a religious island and the last part of the road from the traffic lights goes past several small chapels. Barbados covers 166 square miles and there are more than forty different religious sects in the island. The majority are non-conformist and there is not much to choose between a great many of them, and there are also the conventional Anglican and Roman Catholic churches. The Bajans have a deep sense of religious conviction. The whole island goes to church on Sunday and the children have a religious upbringing. Every Sunday the children walk in groups to church in spotless starched white bonnets and dresses, clutching their prayer books. The women transform themselves on Sundays too. They wear heavily starched full dresses with stiff petticoats which come down well below the knee and they are "Sunday best" which the poorer English women used to wear years ago. They are so out of place to be ridiculous and yet at the same time they look dignified and impressive. These dresses come out of the same sort of dingy houses that surround Worrell's Meat Depot.

Being so small it is easy to see the whole of Barbados. It takes less than a day to drive round the island and see the main places of interest. A large part of the beauty of the West Indies comes from the tropical vegetation and the wide and exciting range of colours it produces. Barbados has a smaller rainfall than most of the Caribbean islands and therefore the vegetation is not quite so rich as elsewhere, but maybe because of the island's size and because I had a longer time there than anywhere else I was more aware of its beauty.

Poinsettia, bougainvillea, hibiscus and oleander in every little village and in many streets in Bridgetown produced constant flashes of scarlet, yellow, orange and purple. These flowers grow naturally and they make any house however poor look cheerful and welcoming. In the country the Royal palms stand high and erect at the corners of the sugar fields. The Royal palm is well worth its name for it is one of the most regal of all trees. In Barbados it is known, at first it seems almost disrespectfully, as the Cabbage palm. At the top of the trunk under the fronds the first few feet of the bark peels off and hangs down in a cluster in the shape of a cabbage. All along the beaches on the West Coast there are Mancineel trees growing out of the sand, so near the water that a big wave will splash round the bottom. They are reasonably large trees built on mean lines, but down by the water's edge they provide valuable shade. But the Mancineel is just another tree except for its branch structure. The boughs leading off the main trunk soon taper into branches and underneath the sparse foliage there is a maze of small branches. The bark is very wrinkled to give the tree a more venerable appearance than it deserves and set against the night sky it is another impressive example of nature in the tropics. There is a fine example of a Mancineel tree beside a dance floor in the Paradise Beach Club. But it is not a tree from the Garden of Eden because it sheds small green apples which are poisonous and it is dangerous to sit underneath a Mancineel when it is raining. The water which drops off the leaves onto the skin causes blisters.

Another tall, handsome tree with full green foliage is the Pride of India and there are mahogany trees and breadfruit trees which have dark green glossy leaves. Ebony trees are very common and in Barbados they are known as "Woman's tongue" as when the wind blows the small brown pods under the leaves make a loud chattering noise. The most important tree of all is the bearded fig tree which has given its name to Barbados. It is another large tree with a wispy, creeper-like beard which hangs down in thin strands round the trunk. Because of the small rainfall in Barbados there is not much fruit, especially citrus fruit.

For such a small island Barbados has very contrasting scenery on the two sides of the island. While the West Coast is lush and tropical the Atlantic coast is barren and bleak. There, the cliffs are high and it is very windy, the sand is yellow and the waves beat fiercely against the shore, in many places so fiercely that bathing is too dangerous. The coastline is sparsely populated with just a few villages and there is the occasional hotel surrounded by its own cluster of buildings. It is an interesting coastline to see and the country around is attractive and completely unspoilt.

I was driven round the island by Gibbons whose card describes him quite correctly as "a courteous and efficient taxi driver". Gibbons is a small man with a moustache and a green homburg hat and he is not given to saying much, but what he does say has been carefully considered. Gibbons spends most of the year on the taxi rank at the Blue Waters Hotel, but he is also Jim Swanton's personal taxi driver when he is in Barbados and staying at his house I used him a great deal and there is a no more splendid character on the island. He is no great mechanic and his car was often near the point of death.

"Yes sir," he would say slowly, "I think it is the clutch."

On some days he would arrive in a friend's car while his own was being put right and he would never let one down. Gibbons like most Bajans has a great sense of humour although he chuckles rather than laughs. He has a gold shirt and a black bow tie which he wears on "big occasions". Gibbons was an excellent guide for he knew a lot about Barbados and if ever he was uncertain of his facts he would stop the car, disappear and come back five minutes later with someone who knew the answer.

Gibbons was typical of so much that is Barbados. The

charm, the old world courtesy, the leisurely approach to life and the reflective atmosphere of the island. It was sad for the Bajans that they should see the dullest Test of the series for Barbados is the spiritual home of cricket in the West Indies and deserved better. On the other hand it was a sleepy game of cricket which fitted in well with the least volatile and most undemonstrative of the West Indian people I met.

There was drama before the Test for Titmus, Cowdrey's vice-captain, lost four toes when he got drawn into a speed boat propeller and the redoubtable Lock was flown out from Perth, Western Australia as a replacement, but not in time to play in this match. This time Sobers won the toss and at three minutes to eleven Cowdrey and his team followed the umpires onto the field and when Camacho and Nurse were in position the proceedings began. They were both in the mood for siege warfare and at lunch two hours later after thirty overs the West Indies were 37 for no wicket and five of these were no balls. It was that sort of game. There was any amount of nondescript cricket and the match was not stamped with individual character in the way of the other four. There was a vivid flash of Sobers, a rugged and determined effort by Edrich which went on for more than seven and three-quarter hours and some exciting strokeplay on the last day by Lloyd when the match was already dead. The game flickered briefly to life in the half an hour before lunch on the final day when England had a faint hope of victory, but otherwise it plodded uneventfully along. It contained too some incomprehensible pieces of cricket. Why did Camacho bat nearly six hours for 57? Was he given any instructions? Why did Sobers continue to bat at number six? Why did the England batsmen go so slowly on the fourth evening? Maybe the teams were just taking it easy and they were entitled to one bad match out of four, but all through both sides showed a strange reluctance to try and win. Anyway the groups of Bajans in the rum shops every evening during the match discussed all these points and as often as not, came up with worthwhile answers. It is an island where the population "knows" its cricket.

Kensington Oval is the only one of the West Indian grounds which is not enclosed by stands and its openness gives the atmosphere of a club ground and however extreme the interest of the crowd the game does not seem to have the same urgency about it as when it is played on the others. The small Pavilion is also more suitable for a club cricket ground than a Test ground, but all the same it is a Pavilion of great character and is heavily steeped in the tradition of cricket. Over the bar upstairs there is a photograph of Frank Worrell, Everton Weekes and Clyde Walcott sitting on the grass in front of the Pavilion at a time when Gary Sobers was a small boy. Any Pavilion which has nurtured these four and many others besides must give off a strong aura of cricket.

King Dyall is another important Kensington landmark. He is as famous a cricketing figure there as anyone who puts on white flannel trousers. The King, an elderly Bajan, comes to watch the cricket in bright and immaculately cut shark skin suits and he holds an elegant silver topped cane and wears fanciful shoes. On the first day of this Test his suit was purple, his shoes white and he wore a topee. Old age has dimmed his flamboyance, but he is still a colourful figure who starts the day at the back of the Pavilion where he wishes everyone good morning with meticulous care. The King helps the sense of occasion and through the day as he watches intently there is a constant stream of smoke from his pipe.

Most of the immediate excitement in this Test was provided by the school children from their special stand to the left of the Pavilion. For most of the game they maintained an ear-splitting crescendo and when right at the bitter end Charlie Griffith advanced and drove Pocock for six, their rendering of "Glory, Glory, Alleluja" must have been audible in St. Lucia.

I was in Gibbons' hands that day driving round the island and we started by going back into Bridgetown and out the other side through the cane fields. Soon we were at Hackleton's Cliff high above the Atlantic looking down on a rough and windswept coastline which is amazingly un-West Indian and yet is barely twenty miles from Sandy Lane. The Crane Hotel, one of the oldest on the island, is on a neighbouring cliff, but the hotels in this part have been superseded for ever by the West Coast Hotels. The condition of the paintwork showed this and had been so for some time.

From here onwards there are famous landmarks every fifteen miles or so round the island. St. John's Church, the original being built in 1640 by the Duke of Monmouth's supporters who had been exiled by Oliver Cromwell. The Red Legs or poor whites as they are known have survived, but they have not intermarried and the strain has been badly weakened by constant inter-breeding and they are now only fit to do the simplest of manual jobs. They all live in the Parish of St. John's.

The Regency Gothic Castle built by the buccaneer Sam Lord and now turned into a hotel, Sam Lord's Castle, is the next stopping point. Lord used it as his headquarters and it is a remarkable structure to come across in a remote corner of Barbados. Then it is on to Codrington College in Bathsheba, a hilly district known by the early English settlers as "Little Scotland". There is a magnificent avenue of Royal Palms leading down to the theological college. The road becomes more difficult before Farley Hill, an old colonial plantation house where part of the film, *Island in the Sun*, was shot, but since then it has been gutted by fire. Sugar plantations stretch round this area for miles and the chimneys of the old sugar factories rise high into the air at intervals although most are closed, there now being one big factory in each area.

Scenically, Barbados is not dramatically exciting, but this contrast between one coast and the other on such a small island is interesting. The Atlantic coastline is stark and except for the temperature it is similar to parts of the coastline in East Anglia. It is fascinating to come across an Anglican church with an interesting historical background in the middle of rural Barbados. But my overruling impression after a day going round the island was not of the beauty of the buildings I saw or of the country or the coastlines, but the simplicity and charm of the life in the villages we passed through. However beautiful a country maybe it is the people who determine the atmosphere and Barbados, especially the rural area has an atmosphere which seems to say, "Leave me alone, I like it as I am."

The sugar strike had ended during the previous week and on the Sunday I went round the island the villagers were cutting their own small plots of cane near their houses so that

the cane could be taken to the factory early the next
morning. This went on unhurriedly but efficiently behind
and at the side of the houses. If the children were not playing
cricket in the roads they were running about chewing pieces
of cane. The women stood arms folded outside their houses
talking to each other and in some villages there were groups
of small children walking hand in hand in their best clothes
on the way to church. Occasionally, Gibbons had to slow up
to pass a load of cane which was being pulled by horse to
some general loading place. In St. Philip's we passed a
blacksmith's shop which looked exactly like any other
blacksmith's shop I have ever seen.

Barbados has become the home of West Indian cricket and
appropriately a game of cricket, however makeshift was going
on wherever there were more than four or five houses
together. It was played either in the road or on a hopelessly
bumpy piece of ground at the side of the road. They used
makeshift stumps usually three empty Banks' beer bottles
and a roughly hewn bat, but it was played with tremendous
enthusiasm. In one village three children were standing in the
road trying to make a bat out of a piece of the bark of a
cabbage palm which is as hard as most woods. In another
village there was a "match" going on in a dip to the left of
the road. The wicket was in the middle of what at the most
could only have been half an acre. It looked the right length
and from the marks it was used a great deal. The
concentration of the batsman was intense and mid-wicket
chased the ball the three yards before it ran into the long
grass as if his life depended on it. More surprisingly, the
strokes were all pure cricket strokes. Hooking, driving or
cutting the batsman's feet were in the right position and he
was perfectly balanced as he hit the ball. There was no
haphazard slogging and there were some appreciative
spectators. Many of the stars of Barbados cricket have come
from equally poor families and like the boys I saw, they
played cricket first as a game of instinct and as a game of
science when margins for error are increased later on at
higher and more sophisticated levels.

I stopped and talked to one group of cricketers and their
knowledge of the England players and their strengths and
weaknesses was remarkable. Of course Sobers was their hero,

but Graveney did not come far behind. One unusually tall man who spoke fast even by West Indian standards was certain that Knott should keep wicket instead of Parks. He had not seen either, but from listening to the wireless and talking to his friends he had no doubt as to whom was the better wicket-keeper. "Man, the best keeper must play. You cannot afford to give Gary two chances," which was good sense. When they talk about Sobers it is almost as if they are talking about their religion. They do not pronounce Gary as if it had two r's in it, but they say "Gahry" and it makes him sound even more inscrutable.

One of the most delightful scenes that Gibbons and I came across that day was in a small village in St. John's where at the side of a house a man was sitting on a stool with a white towel over his shoulders and he was having his hair cut. The same scene would not have been out of place in any remote village in England.

We passed several churches which were full of people and as in the heat they have no windows, the singing and chanting could be heard a long way off. In church the Bajans sing their hymns and say their responses as though they mean them. Two little chapels we passed were full to the extent that people were sitting outside on the steps and inside cymbals were being played as loud as they could be. There was no discernible tune, but a tremendous noise and the congregation were literally shouting, not singing. It was as though the world was ending and everyone inside was involved in it. Gibbons failed me for the first time as he did not know the name of the sect, but they certainly made an eerie noise. One of the churches called itself the Berean Bible church and the last we passed was for Jehovah's Witnesses, but there were many others in-between.

Although I had my pocket picked in a big crowd coming out after a calypso show in the Globe Theatre, Bridgetown there is not much crime in the island. When I arrived on December 27th the whole island had been badly shaken by two horrible murders early on Christmas morning. An Anglican priest somewhere on the West Coast was celebrating Midnight Mass when two youths broke into his house and tied up his wife who was having a baby, and his small daughter while they ransacked the house. They tied them both very tightly and they soon suffocated and died. Everyone I talked to was visibly shaken by it and my maid in the Marine Hotel summed up the feelings of the island when she said to me, "It ruined Christmas for all of us, and for the Good Lord too." There is still a death penalty in Barbados and most people were content that it should be allowed to serve its purpose.

One offshoot of tourism in Bridgetown is Harry's Nitery which is the most gloriously infamous spot in the Caribbean. It is an advanced and, depending which way you look at it, sophisticated strip club. It has become an internationally known part of Barbados and after a little to drink it can also be the funniest place in the West Indies. Harry himself is a rich character. He introduces his girls as they come on to do their act and has a preamble for each act. His accent comes suavely from Oxford and he is one of the important figures on the island—for the tourist industry anyway. At intervals he is had up on charges of living on immoral earnings or of procuring or whatever. Soon after I arrived in December he was in court on a charge and he was found guilty, but the judge sent him to prison for one day, adding that this would be the day and the sentence would end when the court rose which it did two minutes later.

Barbados is the perfect holiday island. The hotel life which is all that most people want is glorious, but it is also well worthwhile looking beyond.

6

Unspoilt and unaffected

After the turmoil of a Test Match it would be hard to imagine anywhere more refreshing than St. Lucia. The island is completely unspoilt, the scenery is beautiful, the people are delightfully unaffected and the cricket ground on a plateau at the top of Castries has mountains on two sides and a mango grove on a third. It was the first time an MCC side had ever visited St. Lucia and the enthusiasm was remarkable even for the West Indies.

As we circled the bay the mountains rose up on the right and in the far distance, the red roofs of Castries peered through the trees and a banana boat was making its way into the harbour. I was staying at the East Winds Inn which was about six miles from Vigie Airport. The taxi driver spoke in a soft rhythmical accent which was more accustomed to speaking the French dialect than English. Soon we were driving through banana groves with the bunches hanging under the trees from their tough twisted cords. Then it was round to the left where two old car tyres piled on top of each other served as a traffic island. The road was near the coast and we passed a small island about a quarter of a mile from shore which boasted one house. Then we went back inland and on the right the country opened up in great undulating folds of green which were eventually stopped by the mountains in the far distance.

At last the car slowed and we turned left up a road which was like a rough cart track. We bumped our way and ahead and below there suddenly appeared a line of six small hexagonal buildings, a bungalow to the left of them and on the edge of the sea was a low open building. It was a setting which was pure Robinson Crusoe. For six nights I dined in the open building by the sea which was little more than a raised lean-to and each night I ate lobster which had been grilled on charcoal. One evening when the sea was rough during dinner my ankles were submerged by waves, as they broke through the dining room. This happened quite often and it helped to make it the most fascinating hotel I have ever stayed in. The only snag was the sand flies, but in my room there was a spray which I squirted over myself and I was not bitten.

The hexagonal buildings had a bedroom and a shower and a kitchen and a fridge in each. The door and the windows were made out of louvred wood and when it was windy there was a splendid noise as it blew through the room. There was nothing better than lying in bed in those surroundings, looking out at the tropical night sky. In the morning I had breakfast on a small round table outside the door on the little circle of paving stones. There was a hill rising up on one side, the sea was fifty yards away and there were some young palms planted in the grass between the buildings.

A new pavilion had been built on the attractive Victoria Park ground for our visit and there was a crowd on the first day of getting on for 10,000. During the afternoon the crowd by the stand at square leg began to chant each time the bowler ran up and when the batsman played his shot it ended in a great roar. At a party that night a St. Lucian girl asked me if I had heard them chanting. I said I had and she told me excitedly that she had been one of them.

When the bowler starts his run in they shout, "balang, balang, balang", and it gets louder as he nears the crease. Then when the batsman hits his ball they shout, "egas". I asked her what it meant and she told me it was just a form of excitement, but a little later she told someone else about it and he said he had heard that "egas" meant something rather worse than "son of a bitch"

"Oh no," she said pursing her lips and shaking her head. "If someone fell down here now," she went on, pointing beside her, "I would shout 'egas'," she hesitated, "but then I would feel very ashamed." And she grinned sheepishly.

I have never met people so pleased to see us as the St. Lucians. Nothing was too much trouble. All the dignitaries in St. Lucia had large parties for us and on these occasions protocol was at its most extreme. The Governor lived on the Morn which is the big hill overlooking Castries harbour. It was a wonderful view and while we were standing on the lawns in the evening *The France* which we had followed from Bridgetown slipped anchor, while down on the right a Geest banana boat was being loaded. The Premier, pronounced "Preemier" in the island gave a cocktail party which turned into a dance in his house overlooking Vigie Airport. He told me it was very useful as he sent his luggage round by road, but he never left the house himself until his aeroplane had landed and then he walked across the runway. There was something faintly Gilbertian about St. Lucian society although everyone was extremely hospitable.

Looking down from the Morn, Castries seemed a delightfully fresh city with its colourful roofs and a mass of green foliage between each, but the middle of the town was little different from any other in the West Indies. The dusty streets were full of bicycles and people brushed past on the pavement talking their own patois which has a gay and exciting sound. It is easy to recognise several French words which have hardly changed, but when I spoke French back to them they looked at me with blank faces. It is a language which is purely spoken and when I asked a man how he spelt certain words he did not know. The words are basically French, but the grammar is African and normal French means nothing to them. Like the French though they make good use of their hands when they are speaking. When two St. Lucians meet each other in the street or in a shop or maybe at a cricket match, the first one to speak will say, *saccofait* which more or less means, "What are you doing?" to which the other one will reply *moila* which is pronounced "Moyla" and means "I am there." It is a delightfully inconsequential start to any conversation, but it is used all the time and is very nearly French. We had a long discussion about the spelling and it was eventually agreed without any prompting that this was right.

I expected the middle of Castries to be old and colonial, but the main streets are full of big modern stores with high quality goods. It was rather surprising to find them in this situation and also it was surprising that they should do so well. St. Lucia has a small population and although Castries is the only town of any size there are people living in the outlying districts and in a country where the roads are so bad that it takes nearly two and a half hours to drive the 45 miles from the other airport, Beane Field, into Castries, it is not very easy to nip into Castries for a day's shopping. Also the majority of St. Lucians walking about in Castries did not look as if they had the money to go and shop in smart stores.

The second day we were in the island I went into the biggest of these to try and buy myself some cotton trousers. The demand for cotton trousers was obviously small and I was shown from the shirt counter to the underwear counter to the shoe counter before I eventually got to trousers. They had none that I wanted, but while I was looking at their selection a middle-aged male shop assistant who was helping me asked me if I was with the MCC. Then he told me that I should be both proud of and grateful for my heritage. For a quarter of an hour he told me what a splendid job the English had done in the West Indies and how much he admired them. He lectured me on how I should continue to uphold the traditions of the English for which they in St. Lucia were so grateful. He made a long speech and every word of it was felt. He told me too that nearly all St. Lucians felt like this and he hoped that the day when St. Lucia was no longer English would never come. By the end I was almost beginning to feel embarrassed. It was splendid to hear such un-equivocable support for the English and appreciation for what they had done. This was particularly so as in some of the other islands I had met people who had made some very justifiable complaints.

One of the great characters in St. Lucia was Mr. Desir, the Mayor of Castries whom I met late one night at a party. A small man with a tremendous sense of humour, he was the first Mayor of Castries for 111 years and he asked me to go and visit him in his parlour the next morning before cricket started. I duly appeared at ten o'clock and was given rum and coconut water to drink. There were several other people there and Mr. Desir told us amid plenty of laughter about St. Lucia and Castries and his duties.

We were in St. Lucia for six nights, but transport around the island was difficult to arrange. I could not take the whole day off and so saw much less of the island than I would have liked. The best known scenery in St. Lucia are the two "pitons". They are two vast pyramids of rock which come out of the sea just off the coast. I flew over them twice when we landed at Beane Field airport on the journey to and from Jamaica. But at the moment St. Lucia is undeveloped and unspoilt. There are three good hotels in the island, all near Castries and not enough tourists to have changed the tempo of life, or indeed the charm and innocent enthusiasm of the people. This may not be so for very much longer for one remote corner of the island is going to be developed into a super-luxurious tourist resort. As it is now, St. Lucia is the tropical island of everyone's dreams.

There was a rum shop at the end of the drive leading up to the East Winds Inn and on the way to the Premier's party we asked the taxi driver who was called Nelson, if the locals would be pleased to see us. He assured us they would be, so we stopped and went in. There were five or six people outside and as many inside. It was a two roomed wooden hut and even in as remote a place as this there were bright advertisements for soft drinks stuck on the outside. We bought the people inside some rum and they grinned at us, but they spoke only the patois and could not understand English. They kept on raising their glasses to us and grinning. The girl who served us asked me if I wanted the dark or the white rum. I said I would have the white and she spoke to the others in their own language and they all looked at me and laughed so I told her to make it a double and they laughed harder. She gave me the chance to smell it before giving it to me and then I realised why they found it so funny. It was fire water and a double measure would either have burnt a hole in my inside or made me very ill. I made her pour it back and settled for a dark rum and coke.

Amazingly in such a remote and tumbledown place as this there was a juke box on the wall. The man who owned the rum shop owned two others and the music was piped to them. It was amusing to hear tunes from the recent English Hit Parade blaring out of a juke box in a remote part of St. Lucia. The owner whose wife was serving behind the bar had been to England and he had a friend in Dulwich. After a long search he found a letter from him, but was disappointed when I said I did not know him. We bought them all some more rum and left amid enthusiastic handshakes and beaming smiles.

The interest in the cricket, MCC v Windward Isles was of course tremendous. The Windward Isles compete in the Shell Shield, but they play most of their matches in Grenada and so the St. Lucians very seldom see any first-class cricket. This and the fact that it was the first visit of an MCC side to the island meant that the match was a big occasion. The beautiful ground was soon crowded and the facilities were very good. Every ball and every stroke was watched with keenness and appreciation and the local side did well.

It was sad for the St. Lucians that rain ruined the last day. But the crowds came to the ground in hope and sat patiently in the stands long after there was any chance of play. Their determination to get things going if there was any possible chance was perfectly illustrated by a woman who after the first storm which saturated the outfield went thirty yards out from the pavilion and began vainly to sweep the grass with a besom and soon she was joined by more. They helped at the ground and when the pitch had been rolled on the two previous days they had all pushed the roller. The brushing may have been standard procedure. It was sad to have to leave St. Lucia behind.

When we returned to Trinidad for the Fourth Test the Queen's Park Oval was still as lovely as ever. The flamboyant trees were not in flower, but the mountains had maintained their exciting range of colours. The population of Port of Spain seemed to be moving a little more slowly and it wore the complacent smile of a people who had been on an immense bender and were feeling that it had all been well worthwhile. 25,000 people held their breath as Sobers' silver coin glistened momentarily in the sun. The heads of the two captains craned anxiously forwards as it fell and then perversely started to roll on its side down the wicket. Cowdrey straightened first and grinning broadly he threatened to thump Sobers. Tails had fallen heads and the West Indies were batting. The crowd went into hysterics.

The Fourth Test which began amid such jubilant West Indian scenes continued for more than four days in the same vein with the West Indies keeping the upper hand, before ending on the Tuesday evening in scenes of general despair as Boycott and D'Oliveira took a seven wicket English victory back with them into the England dressing room. It was a moment full of irony as this had been the first Test in the series where the West Indies had played consistently better cricket than England. They had lost only nine wickets in their two innings and yet it was the Englishmen who were singing victory songs far into the Tuesday night.

The Caribbean was left in dismay and many people had an immediate desire to crucify Sobers whose declaration alone had made this result possible. The West Indies led by 122 in the first innings and when they went in again only six hours were left and the wicket had held up well. They batted without any urgency until 35 minutes after lunch on the last day when Sobers suddenly got out of his chair and clapped his hands and England had been left to score 215 in 165 minutes. As history knows they did it with three minutes and seven wickets to spare. Sobers had acted on an impulse. When the day began the West Indies were 6 for no wicket and at lunch two hours later they were 72 for one which was hardly the rate of a side batting for a declaration.

How could Sobers have done such a thing? There were not many spectators on the last day, but those there were shocked into silence, but the next morning before flying to Guyana I went to buy some records and my taxi driver was delightfully philosophical. With the usual broad, toothy grin he said to me, "Yes, man, in a game of poker you take a chance. Sobers took a chance and he lost. Man, that's all there is to it." But not everyone regarded cricket as a game of poker.

It was a remark which fitted Trinidad and the taxi driver was right for Sobers is that sort of person. His genius is impulsive and extravagant. When he bats he not only consistently succeeds with the unexpected, but he succeeds in the most spectacular style. When he bowls he is capable of taking two wickets in the first over of an innings when only ten minutes before he has taken off his pads after batting for nearly six hours to score 113 not out and save his side as he did after the riots at Sabina Park. At backward short-leg or at mid-off he catches the impossible and alters the course of the match. On the field of play Sobers appears not to acknowledge the impossible for he has no need. It was logical therefore for him to have declared when he did and maybe it was an effront to his genius that he lost. It was a gamble which did not come off. Sobers was unpopular for it and in some places it was obviously felt that he had gambled with nationalism but if the West Indies had won he would have been feted through the entire Caribbean. Because he lost he was roundly condemned.

No man did more than Cowdrey to win this match for England. In the first innings when England were for a long time struggling against the possibility of having to follow-on, he batted methodically, carefully and chancelessly for five hours making 148 and taking his side to safety. Then in the second innings when victory was in front of him, he made 71 in 76 minutes with a succession of brilliant strokes, and virtually won the match for England. These were two amazingly contrasting innings; Cowdrey had first of all saved the match for England and then batting again he won it. Sobers may have given England the chance, but they were good enough to take it.

7

Two countries in one

I found Guyana the most fascinating of all the countries which form the cricketing West Indies. It is the West Indies at the same time as being South America. In Georgetown, a Dutch colonial city, the atmosphere of the islands is strong, but just a mile outside, it becomes a big country. The Demerara river, nearly a mile across more than twenty miles from the mouth, glistens through the trees on the left of the road on the drive from the airport, Atkinson Field, to Georgetown. In the mouth of the Essequibo which is twenty miles across there is an island as big as Barbados. The Kaiteur falls in the interior have a sheer drop of 743 feet and are the tallest in the world. The cathedral in Georgetown is the tallest wooden building in the world and the sea is a dirty brown colour.

At first Georgetown is like so many old colonial cities. The outskirts seem over-populated, the living conditions squalid and there are other obvious signs of poverty, but nearer the middle it gets better. The most noticeable difference between Georgetown and the other West Indian cities I saw was the Dutch influence. It was obvious in the architecture even down to the recently built wooden houses in the poor areas, and also in the layout of the city. In the more prosperous parts the houses were set back further from the road, there was plenty of vegetation and several of the roads still have their contemporary canals running down the middle. Some of them have been filled in so that there is a tarmac path in between wide grass verges between the two carriageways. They help give parts of Georgetown a peaceful almost stately atmosphere.

But Georgetown is a difficult city to stay in. The comforts are few and what hotels there are, are bad. There is only one restaurant worth going to, the Palm Court, but after a while the staple diet of prawn cocktail and steak washed down by Mateus Rose, at a high price, and black coffee becomes monotonous. Most of the beef is home grown by the ranchers in Berbice and in the interior, in the Rupununi. It has a good flavour, but it is tough and this is because the steers run wild and the grazing is not very nourishing and it is at least three years before they are ready to be slaughtered.

There has never, until very recently, been a need for hotels in Georgetown except perhaps during Test matches as there is no tourism. People who live there entertain most handsomely, but almost exclusively in their houses. Because of the living conditions in the hotels—each night there were cockroaches in my bedroom, the lavatory did not often work and the shower was temperamental—it is tempting to write Guyana off. But for those who are prepared to look and see it is rewarding.

Georgetown itself offers all the usual contrasts of new and old, bare existence and thriving commercialism, the ox cart and the Cadillac, Starboek Market and the omnipotent Booker Brothers store. Dingy little streets lead off main thoroughfares and outside the big modern stores which would disgrace no city in the world, elderly women crouch on the pavement at the side of the doors selling various kinds of food as well as biros and combs and bootlaces out of dirty baskets and wooden trays. There would also be several bicycles leaning against the wall—Georgetown is a city of bicycles—a few small children standing staring hand-to-mouth, and a formidable female policeman would probably be hovering around as like as not talking to another vendor. There is a constant flow of people down the pavement. The poorer women stop by the street sellers and bend down to inspect their wares while the better off members of the community funnel into the entrance of the store. A piercing voice tried to sell me some fruit. I shook my head and smiled and instead bought two boxes of matches for ten cents. Then I went inside the store and a smart shop girl tapping about in high heels sold me a bottle of Arden-for-Men for ten dollars.

There are two markets in Georgetown, the Starboek Market and the Bourda Market. Starboek Market is in the centre of the city and although walking through the area there is a mixture of Victorian and Dutch architecture, Starboek built in the 1880's, is a remarkable building suddenly to come across. The clock tower in the front of the building is surmounted by a red pyramid supported by posts on the roof of the clock. The pyramid and the clock are visible through leaves and round corners sometime before one gets to the market. The rest of the building lives up to this impressive start. It is very long and gabled with a facade of white and red painted wood.

Starboek covers a lot of ground. Inside, the stalls are packed tight together and the passageways between the rows were filled with people when I went there one morning. I spent over an hour inside and I could not have seen more than half of it. There are stalls selling clothes, shoes, meat, drink, eggs, flour, sugar and every other conceivable domestic article. Many stalls sold the same wares, but trade seemed good. In the small space behind the counter a woman would be sitting on a box waiting for customers. The men who worked there walked quickly through the passages, sometimes carrying boxes, sometimes stopping to talk and sometimes shouting instructions. It was a daily scene which had happened like this for a long time and was going to go on for a lot longer. The most unpleasant part of it was the smell. The meat counters were hung with flesh which had gone black and dry on the outside and gave off the strong smell of meat which is not very fresh. Around the counters which were selling rough grained flour and something that looked like maize—the smell was sweet and musty. Each type of stall had its own smell and in the heat they were all rather stronger than normal. I did not see another European as I walked through the Market, but whenever I stopped at a counter to look at the goods the people were happy to talk to me and the sellers and other buyers offered me advice. When a man offered to sell me some type of food of which I had never heard I refused, and a group of people who were listening laughed hard. I never discovered what I had missed or if it was my misfortune or the stallholder's. In general, it was a scene which showed the Guyanese women doing their daily shopping in their own way. And it was probably a lot more sanitary than it looked. I was only glad to get away from the smell and the heat.

Bourda Market, partly in the open air and partly under

cover, is very near the cricket ground. Fruit and vegetables are mostly sold here and the sellers line the edges of an area which could not be much more than three acres. It has a more familiar atmosphere than Starboek and in the mornings it was always full of people, and children were running through the crowds playing. And there was as much chatter as action.

I came across one of the most curious sights in Georgetown walking back to my hotel from the Starboek Market. At the side of the pavement behind a loose barbed wire fence a group of Indians were operating a Heath Robinson sugar grinder. There was a lot of cane lying on the ground and at intervals it was being fed onto the top of a contraption on wheels which was a cross between a barrel organ and an ice-cream trolley. At one side, level with the cane was a big wheel which was being worked manually with a wooden canopy over the top. The cane was being ground up in preparation presumably for the process of being turned into sugar and molasses. It was being worked by Indians and when I got close one of them began to smile at me and whenever I said anything he smiled and said, "sugar". With the barbed wire separating us I never got nearer the truth. But it seemed odd to find this sort of operation going on in a country which is highly mechanised for the production of sugar.

Guyana offers several paradoxes. It is a very poor country and yet in the interior there are rich mineral deposits including gold, but there is no money to develop them. The population near the coast is almost entirely African and Indian with the Africans predominating in Georgetown and the Indians grouping outside. But the interior is populated largely by the indigenous Indian tribes, the Amerindians. There are many different tribes, the Wapishana, the Macusi, the Patamona, the Arecuna, the Arawaks and the Wai-Wai are six of them and there are many more. Amerindian is the collective name and is short for American Indian as opposed to East Indian. The Amerindians have much paler skins than the Africans and they are a small people. Their ancestors originally came from Tibet thousands of years ago. They came by land to the Bering straits which separate Russia from

Alaska and having crossed over worked their way slowly down through North America. On the way they picked up a Red Indian strain which is still noticeable.

Guyana has a reputation for riots and internal disorders, but fifteen days in and around Georgetown I found this surprising. The colour question was not more sharply etched than anywhere else and the people were volatile and in a European sense immature, but no more so than in the islands. The trouble is caused by racialism inside the community. The political parties align themselves, one with the Africans and one with the Indians, and at election time clever orators can stir up in one race a hatred of the other. They are not doing this deliberately, but like all politicians they are trying to win votes and in those circumstances almost anything can be said and this is dangerous when the audience consists of highly excitable people. The "riots" in Guyana usually take the form of continual reprisals by one side against the other after the first atrocity had been committed. I talked one evening to the assistant police commissioner who was saying in what a hopeless situation this sort of trouble left the police. They never knew where the next murders or arson were coming from and it could just as easily be the murder of children as of adults. When the riots begin the feelings become intensely bitter, but from walking round Georgetown talking to anyone and everyone, I never came across any sign of fierce racial hatred. But after his declaration at Port of Spain, Sobers was given a police guard outside his hotel which again showed the narrow division between disappointment and resentment with excitable people and in the West Indies this is a fact of life. All nationalities have their own innate characteristics, have to live with them and ultimately learn to overcome them.

Guyana is both the West Indies and South America. In Georgetown the population is largely African mainly because they are still very aware of the slave days and they have therefore a natural antipathy towards working on the land with the memories this invokes.

They have all therefore gravitated to Georgetown where they staff the shops and offices. Also the Africans are naturally more gregarious than the Indians who are mostly found in the fertile belt of land stretching along the coast. I was taken round one of the Booker Brothers sugar estates, La Bonne Intention, and the labour force both in the factory and out in the field was mostly Indian.

In Georgetown the people I talked to about Guyana and its problems all had liberal views towards the future, but on the sugar estate although attitudes have changed greatly from the days of colonialism, it is still a colonial atmosphere. I was taken round the estate standing up in the back of a Land Rover by a field manager who had come across from England as a young man and knew everything there was to be known about growing sugar. Wearing a khaki shirt and shorts and a topee he told me about the problems of irrigation, of harvesting, of starting a new strain of sugar cane. He told me about the sugar contents of the various strains, about the seven year period in which the cane is cut to the roots which then grow again for the next year's crop, about the job after the seventh year of cleaning the field completely and preparing for a new growth. We went through the whole procedure from start to finish and all the time the tall smoking chimney of the factory which somehow looked strangely out of place was visible. His job was growing sugar and getting it down the canals to the factory as efficiently as possible.

I saw fields being cut which had been burnt the night before to destroy the "trash", and simplify the job of cutting. There were fields which had been cleaned in preparation for replanting which were purposefully flooded and then drained before the cuttings were planted. Two fields were in the process of being planted and the workers with their huge razor sharp knives with which they also cut the cane, were slicing cuttings off big canes which were grown for this purpose. It was fascinating to watch the workers use their knives for they are fierce instruments which could cause severe injuries. Yet they use them quickly and efficiently and they take great pride in their knives. They have to provide their own and each night they are carefully cleaned. A cane worker without a knife is not a cane worker.

Driving down the long causeways surrounded by channels for transporting the sugar to the factory and by wide irrigation channels which at times cross over each other, the green sugar cane rippled in the wind for as far as I could see. Sugar production was going on as it had for years. Efficiency was everything and the labour force had to be carefully controlled. The ways of the plantocracy were inevitably not conducive to liberal thinking.

We drove around the estate for two hours and going down one causeway I was lucky enough to see an anteater. About fifty yards ahead a long black creature with a big bushy tail ran across the track. It must have been at least four feet long from head to tail and it had a narrow, angry face. They are fierce animals, but are seldom seen. This one was probably on the move because some fields had been burnt the previous evening in preparation for cutting and the anteater had been driven across the estate.

The morning I spent at La Bonne Intention was kindly arranged for me by Edgar Readwin, the Chairman of the sugar side of Bookers in Guyana and it was a fascinating experience. Guyana is one of the few countries which has two sugar crops a year, but the cane has a low sugar content and the production methods and the trade unions which govern the labour force ensure a high production cost, which is only just competitive.

It is the African population which makes Georgetown so strongly West Indian. All over the West Indies the Africans have lived outside their indigenous environment for so long that they have naturally adapted themselves to the islands or countries of their enforced adoption and have become indigenous to their new environments. The Africans in the different islands have acquired the characteristics of their islands and are therefore rather different in each. Also they came originally from different tribes in Africa and some of the basic characteristics of the individual tribes are still there. But the Africans also have characteristics which are common to them all. One of these is an urge for spontaneous enjoyment. In this respect the Guyanese Africans are the same as all the other West Indian Africans I met.

Georgetown was our last port of call and the biggest manifestation of this was once more calypso and the Mighty Sparrow. He came over from Trinidad with the cricketers to do two or three shows in Georgetown and others in Berbice.

On every door, on every lamp post, on every hoarding in Georgetown were posters advertising the Sparrow Spectacular. When I saw him in the Pavilion at Bourda Oval he gave me two box tickets for his show at the Globe Theatre.

It must have been about the tenth time I had seen Sparrow in the West Indies, but it was the most exciting show of all. The front few rows in the balcony were divided into boxes and we were there at ten past seven. Downstairs the seating was full and there were people clamouring to be let in at all the doors. I could not see another European upstairs although the light was dim and there may have been a few. The seats filled up around us with girls in bright dresses mostly with their hair piled high on their heads. For the men it was open-necked shirts and cotton trousers and it was still too hot.

Only the front part of the stage was being used and on the left hand side there were instruments and stools waiting to be filled by a local group for the opening of the evening. The Master of Ceremonies, Mr. Habeeb Khan, came running onto the stage every two minutes and ten minutes before the start an electrician put up a folding ladder at the side of the stage and mended a light. Then two or three minutes before the start the doors were opened and a mass of people came flooding down the gangways below where they stood pressed tight together for the whole performance. The programme printed the words of four of Sparrow's calypsos including 'Mister Walker' and then on the middle pages, a list of the performers.

It was twenty to eight before the "Young Ones" settled down to produce their idea of pop. The lead guitarist had obviously been watching films, they do not have television in Guyana, for he jumped about and tapped his feet and generally "looked the part". The second guitarist was a figure of intense concentration. His head was bent close over the strings and he would not have been an ideal performer for "Top of the Pops". They were not very good, at least to English ears, but as a pipe opener they were well received. Mr. Habeeb Khan then pranced on, grabbed a microphone and announced the Vasso de Freitas Ork as they were billed in the programme. He announced them and turned round to the entrance with open arms, but this bit had not been

rehearsed very well for the Ork missed their cue and came
slowly on in ones and twos talking to themselves. But it did
not matter. The audience would have laughed at anything
and this lack of polish seemed to make the whole evening
that much more friendly and spontaneous.

The Ork played themselves in before Mr. Habeeb Khan
returned and announced the first of the calypsonians, Lord
Zandolie. He came bouncing out wearing a loud brown
checked coat which was two sizes too small, grinned
profusely, danced around the stage and sang about the man
who kept "the biggest cock in the island". The audience
collapsed into hysterics and unfortunately I did not hear a
word. Lord Zandolie did a hip-waggling exit and his place was
taken by the sprightly Lord Laro who went straight into 'the
Betting Contest' which was a calypso about an American, a
Trinidadian and a girl. The Trinidadian won but quite how I
never found out as the punch lines produced pandemonium.

In the front row of the stalls there was a big man wearing
a white shirt and a large panama hat. He never took it off and
during 'the Betting Contest' he turned round to those behind
laughing so that his teeth flashed even in this light. He spent
the last two verses on his feet and at every joke he bent down
and slapped his thigh. The audience laughed at him and with
him, but they made no attempt to restrain him. It was all
part of the evening. Lord Laro was followed by the elegant
Lord Shorty. He wore a bright, close fitting giraffe-coloured
suit and all six foot six of him, he might have been taller,
came languidly onto the stage looking exactly like a giraffe.
His trousers were far too short, but he had on a magnificent
pair of light blue socks which more than made up for the
deficiency. Lord Shorty sent my nextdoor neighbour into
hysteria with one number on the usual boy meets girl theme.

After Lord Shorty there was a pause and as Mr. Habeeb
Khan was running about with a frown on his face—something
was obviously wrong. Then the light at the side of the stage
went out. The electrician came on with his folding ladder and
got it to work again. By the entrance on the right hand side
of the stage there was a girl in pink standing and watching
and she stayed throughout the show. There were several
others around who came on stage to watch one performer
and then drifted away. No one minded and the electrician

having been brought on had no intention of leaving. He pushed his ladder into the corner and stood where he was. Another permanent fixture was a middle-aged man in a bright yellow shirt and a white cap who was sitting nearly in the middle of the stage and enjoying himself enormously. Later in the evening the light on the other side of the stage went out.

Lord Shorty went as slowly as he had come and now there were two invitation calypsonians who were not in the programme. First it was a Lordship in a brown suit and tie and a bowler hat. He was followed by Lord.Blakie who is the playboy among the aristocratic calypsonians. He ran on in a shining white suit with a bright pink tie and sang about the pros and cons of girls in a loud resonant voice. Then it was Lord Canary and by now it was clear that the calypsonians needed decolonising. Lord Canary was Guyana's own Calypso King and he got a tremendous reception. With considerable polish he sang 'The Wicked Cricket Match'. It is a calypso about a man and a woman who play a single wicket cricket match. I only heard a few of the words, but enough to buy the record the next morning although I still cannot hear them all. The audience went mad and were reluctant to let him go. At last he withdrew and a man who had been standing in a side gangway walked out in front of the stalls, unfolded his handkerchief, laid it carefully on the floor before sitting on it. Maybe he had a stitch.

We now had a break from calypso. The Guyana Jokers, African dancers, appeared and were neither good nor funny. They were followed by Krishna, an Indian dancer who was politely received by an audience which was eagerly awaiting more calypsos. When he had finished Mr. Habeeb Khan appeared and gave the next performer whose name sounded something like Aly Khan a big build up. We were told that he was the funniest man in Guyana and that it was a great privilege for us that he should be with us. He was not on the programme. When the moment came for his entrance the Vasso de Freitas Ork appeared in ones and twos. Mr. Habeeb Khan had a worried conversation with Vasso de Freitas and the Ork withdrew. Then the eagerly awaited Aly Khan appeared with a series of quick-fire "jokes". He did everything except thank the audience for the rapturous applause after the first three had been received in silence. He went on for a long time keeping his *tour de force* which was the most gloriously obscene and obvious part of the evening to the end.

Now it was back to calypso and the finale which the audience could hardly wait for. Calypso Rose burst on in a bright shiny red suit with a white blouse and a considerable bust. She gave a masterful performance of her 1967 Carnival Winner, 'Fire in your Wire'. She is a big woman with a deep voice and dancing round the stage singing, 'Fire, fire in your Wire, Wire!' she almost had the roof off. She was full of personality and while on stage seemed to own it and her presentation of this calypso was strikingly effective. It was up in the higher reaches of the calypso Debrett with the Mighty Duke the 1968 Carnival Calypso King. Resplendent in coronet he sang his best known calypso, 'What is Calypso?' It tells the story of the origin of the calypso and it has a haunting melody which is strengthened by the Mighty Duke's precise and controlled voice. He had this noisy audience silent and listening as he sang, but he was unlucky to be appearing just before the Mighty Sparrow as he did not get the reception he deserved.

The Mighty Sparrow was the only commoner among the male calypsonians. Yet in his immaculate white dinner jacket he was every inch a lord. Sparrow takes command of a stage the moment he appears. He is the only big calypsonian who does nothing else but sing calypsos. Out of the calypso season the others all do different jobs, but Sparrow's whole life is calypso. He works at it hard and he is much the most polished performer of all. I met a man who had seen him in a show with Sammy Davis Junior in America and he said Sparrow came second but not by so very much. On stage Sparrow's movements are controlled, he has a good voice and he puts his calypsos across with great polish.

He sang five calypsos. None of the first four was 'Mister Walker' and with the audience waiting for this one, Sparrow got little more than polite applause for each of them. The words come across well and he showed his professional touch with the microphone. Some of the others who had used a microphone less than Sparrow were too selfconscious about it. They held it awkwardly and some looked as if they were frightened of it, but Sparrow made the mike fit in with him. When he had finished his fourth calypso all the calypsonians came on stage and stood round Sparrow, and the Ork who played extremely well throughout, burst into 'Mister Walker'. The audience moved with Sparrow. 'Mister Walker' has a strong beat and the whole theatre swayed with it. Sparrow presented it masterfully with the other calypsonians doing the chorus.

MISTER WALKER
Verse 1

She ugly yes
But she wearing them expensive dress
People say she ugly
But she father full ah money
Oh Lord Mama woy woy
Chorus
Good morning Mister Walker
Ah come to see you daughter
Aye Mister Walker
Ah come to see you daughter
Sweet Rosemarie she promise she go marry me
And now ah tired waiting
Ah come to fix the wedding

Verse 2

After the wedding day
Ah don't care what nobody say
Every time ah take ah good look
At she face ah see a bank book
Oh Lord Mama woy woy

Verse 3

Apart from that
They say that she too big and fat
When she dress they tantalise she
Saying monkey wearing mini
Oh Lord Mama woy woy

Verse 4

All I know
Is that I don't intend to let she go
Cause if she was a beauty
Nothing like me could get she
Oh Lord Mama woy woy

The final chorus ended in a tremendous crescendo. And that was that. It was back to the Palm Court and prawn cocktail and steak etcetera after an unforgettable West Indian evening of uncontrolled fun and enthusiasm. It was the West Indies in Georgetown. It is apparently dangerous to walk through Georgetown at night, but I do not think that any of that audience would have sneaked up on me.

But when England had somehow struggled through the last day of the Fifth Test there was a big crowd in the road behind the Pavilion which threw stones at the Englishmen as they went to their cars. Nothing can be taken for granted. It was suitable that this last Test Match with its dramatic upheavals and contrasts should have taken place in Guyana, a country which seems to combine just about all the moods that this remarkable game passed through.

After a week of mounting tension in which Sobers' declaration in Port of Spain was alternately attacked and defended, another heart was transplanted and Sparrow had hummed the chorus of 'Mister Walker' in the Pavilion at Bourda Oval, the first day arrived. Bourda is a small and very attractive ground. It is surrounded by stands and terracing and it gives the impression of being a big ground in miniature. The scale is right and the stands are in proportion to everything else. It does not have the cramped urgency of Sabina Park and is better organised, but like all West Indian grounds it has its own charm and atmosphere which does nothing to steady the nerves before a Test Match. For the last leg of their tour the English had moved from the land of Coke to the hard stuff. Instead of the usual myriad of Coca-Cola advertisements the ground was full of boards advertising Scotch Whisky. These boards were put up on the popular side and they glared incongruously across on a pleasant white Pavilion which with its green roof and sprawling annexe looked down in a prim and stately way as a Victorian lady might with her skirts down to her ankles. The green-roofed stands around the remainder of the ground were new and spruce and packed to overflowing. The noise and excitement bubbled out of each, just as the lid of a kettle rattles as it boils.

The outfield was the smoothest in the West Indies and the final touch was given by the mounted police who patrolled the boundary on immaculately groomed horses. When play began they took up their positions, one or two in each corner of the ground. They were impressive in their flat white caps and black trousers with a thick red stripe down the outside. The heavy wooden truncheons in leather holsters at the side of the saddle showed that the police were not necessarily there only for display.

After Cowdrey had lost the toss Nurse played and missed at the second ball of Snow's first over and the first ball of Jones's over. The wicket played well to begin with and after the West Indies had lost three wickets for 72 Kanhai and Sobers put on 250, both reaching 150. England soon finished off the innings when they were parted, but after Boycott and Cowdrey had added 172 for the second wicket England collapsed and it was left to Lock to take them to safety with his highest score in first-class cricket. The West Indies began their second innings at breakneck speed already 43 runs ahead. Sobers played another glorious innings failing by only 5 runs to reach his second hundred of the match and the last day was all England's to score 308 or to bat for five and a half hours.

The final day unwound like a skilfully produced drama. England 33 for 0, 41 for 5, 103 for 5, 122 for 5 and Cowdrey 50, 168 for 6 and Cowdrey lbw, Knott 50, 198 for 7 with 25 minutes left, 200 for 8, 206 for 9, six minutes to go and then the last over from Gibbs to Jones. As Gibbs walked back to bowl the last ball of the series and Jones settled over his bat, a lot of people held their breath. The events of the past six days had gone, they were history, this was the agonising present. The result of 27 days Test cricket rested on that last ball and at the end of an incredible tour England were depending on Jones' batting to give them the series.

There were many heroes in this final Test, one was thrown up in almost every session of play. Knott, Cowdrey, Lock,

Boycott were England's principals, but in cricketing terms Sobers's achievement in making 152 and 95 not out as well as taking 3 for 72 and 3 for 53 in 37 and 31 overs was on its own. Sobers had come to Georgetown an unpopular man. He was accused of being selfish, uninterested, irresponsible and other things besides, but on the field of play he had answered his critics singularly and collectively in the most emphatic way. It was staggering that he should have achieved all this without his side winning the match. Kanhai and Gibbs were his two most successful assistants. It was, however, a measure of England's achievement that whereas they had been good enough to win when they had been given the chance at Port of Spain, they were good enough to draw over six days at Georgetown after losing the toss.

It was a match which took the players through just about every emotion that can be aroused on a cricket field. At the end of a long and difficult tour the England players had held on to their emotions, although it was a close thing. The personnel which were fielding on the fifth evening had changed slightly since the First Test, two and a half months earlier and their faces were brown. Jones was still walking the first six paces before breaking into his high-stepping and enthusiastic run up. Lock, a little fatter than of old but just as bald, crouched at short-leg, handkerchief knotted round his neck and when he appealed he let the world know about it as he had always done. Barrington, the great professional, moved quietly into position and Pocock was fielding and throwing as he had never done before. Snow walked lethargically back to long-leg and in again at the end of the over, apparently in a world of his own, but with figures of 6 for 60 to show where he and his heart really were.

Edrich with his tanned face stalked into position at mid-wicket as though he might be back in his native Norfolk at harvest time. Cowdrey going from first slip to first slip was as courteous of movement and manner as he had ever been. Beside him Graveney in a white sun hat moved more elegantly than any and as briskly as most and these two, arms folded, were talking between balls and a lot wiser now than when they had talked at Queen's Park Oval in the middle of January. On the long-leg boundary D'Oliveira stood in the shadows with his hands behind his back staring reflectively into the stand. Maybe he was thinking about that catch at Sabina Park. Behind the wicket Knott, the epitome of youth, was bouncing and smiling, thrilled to be there and loving every minute. And Boycott was just, the dedicated Boycott doing his duty, sun hat, sweat bands and all. Everyone was giving his all as they had done throughout the series, but this was the final throw and the stakes were high.

It was the frenetic excitement of this Test which I left on the Sunday to visit wild South America and a greater contrast than that would be hard to imagine. In Georgetown I met Diane McTurk whose father was one of the earliest English pioneers in the Rupununi. Diane had spent a lot of her life in the interior and hearing her talk about the Amerindian tribes and their customs and the exciting country there is in the interior, I realised that Guyana was more than just the West Indies. She arranged to take me by speedboat that last Sunday up to Santa Mission which is the nearest Amerindian settlement to Georgetown.

We drove out to Atkinson Field to pick up the boat and when we arrived the sky was black and it was raining hard. After a while we decided to brave it and by the time we had carried the picnic hampers the fifty yards to the landing pier we were wet beyond caring. At this point the Demerara is about three quarters of a mile across and with the dark grey clouds overhead, some blue sky on the horizon and the rain beating into the dark water it was a wonderfully impressive sight.

At the top of the wooden steps we had to go down to get into the boat there was a stall which sold rum, Pepsi-Cola, several other kinds of drink and cigarettes and there were some people standing around. Our boat had been laid on by the captain of the police at Atkinson and although he could not be there to organise things we were expected and well looked after. Our pilot was a small thick-set young man wearing a white shirt, who obviously had a lot of Amerindian blood in him.

It was still raining when we set off and the pilot gave us a waterproof rug, but it was unnecessary by then and in any case there was a perspex wind shield. The far bank of the Demerara looked a long way off as we drew out into the river. We went upstream diagonally across the river to the entrance of the Kimuné tributary which was well wooded and I could not make it out until we were nearly to it. The tributary was never more than seventy yards across and mostly a good deal less. As we entered it with the foliage and the scrub coming down right to the water's edge and a bend just in front, it was like entering a new world. When we were round the bend I looked back and the wash from the boat was the only influence human beings had had on the world I could see. The tributary was an endless succession of bends and soon the light dimmed as the trees came down to the water and rose high above so that we were nearly enclosed with only a thin line of sky between the tree tops. The water was steely black and the tide was going out. Our pilot knew the Kimuné well and the course to steer round each bend. The big logs, visible and dangerous only when the tide is out, were a reminder of what might have happened if he had lost his way although there were no crocodiles. Weeds were the other hazard and twice the propellers got badly bound up. The first time the pilot's assistant at the back quickly cleared them, but it took much longer the second time and with the engine stopped and the tide going fiercely out we were swept backwards almost as fast as we had been going forwards. At last it was cleared and we were off again. Round each bend a straight piece of water opened out and in its steely blackness, the trees and the sky were perfectly mirrored. There was not a ripple in front of us and the engine made a harsh, unreal noise. The huge clumps of bamboo with the individual pale coloured bamboo sticks splaying out and upwards like the cords of some giant parachute were fascinating. Their reflection glistened out of the water and by the time I had looked up at the bamboo and then back at the water some other reflection had taken its place. Every corner was exciting and the colours set against the still, shining black surface were magical.

We did not see many birds although round one corner when we were out of the thickest of the forest and were now surrounded by swamp land, a pair that looked and flew like highly coloured magpies flapped across the water. They were Spur Wings and had striking brown and yellow wings with spurs on the end. They use the spurs which are pieces of bone to hitch themselves up on branches. There was also a

Blue Crane which flies and looks very like an English Heron. Later on there were some pigeons which were unmistakeable and some "Blackbirds" which were like all-black magpies. They are known locally as "Old Witches". We did not go far enough into the interior to see any wild Canjé pheasants which are very beautiful highly coloured birds. The Canjé, known as Stinking Hanna because they give off a revolting smell, have reached a strange stage of evolution for they can hardly fly and they can only flap awkwardly about in the mangroves.

The swampland stretched most of the way to the Mission. There was a lot of tall grass, some clumps of scrub and at well spaced intervals the splended Ité palms looked proudly down. They are huge palm trees which are very like the Royal palms in Barbados. We passed a landing stage and on the bank at the next corner stood a large silk cotton tree with its thick silvery trunk and its bushy foliage right at the top. Wherever I looked on this journey there was something new to see and although we were very near to the coast, Diane told me that this stretch of river was very similar to the rivers deep in the interior and in the Amazon country itself.

We came down one long straight stretch and the pilot throttled back as we passed two small boats of children who were fishing and up on a hill to the left the Mission building showed through the trees. On the right bank the swamp stretched away for ever with the tall Ité palms doing sentry duty over the area. We came slowly into the landing stage where there were some children and an old man watching us. As we climbed ashore I put my cupped hand in the shallow water which was dark brown and when I looked closely at the water I saw it was genuinely dark brown and there was no sediment. Before our things were carried up the hill Diane talked to the old man who had watched us land. She told him she had spent much of her life in the Rupununi and they talked about the Amerindian customs and the old man was delighted to talk to someone who understood his way of life. As they went on, his distinguished weather-beaten face creased into a grin and he promised to take us round the Mission when we had finished lunch.

We eventually decided to eat sitting on the large roots of a handsome tree which stood at the top of the hill. The tree which looked very like a silk cotton tree was called a Stinking Toe tree. Diane had brought a large thermos picnic container and we sat under the Stinking Toe drinking a bottle of cold Reisling which was an unlikely situation. When we had finished lunch we took the dirty plates and what was left of the food down to the boat and Diane said that anyone could have what was left if they would do the washing up in exchange. A small boy who was the headman's son was given the food which he took home while someone else did the washing up. Then we joined the old man.

"Are you interested in cricket?" Diane asked him.

"No, I am afraid not," he shook his head apologetically. We were no longer in the West Indies.

Santa is a mission for a tribe of Arawak Indians. We saw a lot of children and while we were having lunch two girls who must have been about fifteen walked past us. They were dressed in European clothes and when they saw us they looked neither frightened nor inquisitive. There were several women about, but except for a few of the elderly, no men as they were all away working on the "grants". The Guyanese government allots certain areas to people as timber grants which mean that they can cut and sell the timber. The labour is done by the Amerindians and so the men leave their villages and live on the "grant", returning home three times a year to the mission. The headman is elected as head of the village when the previous headman becomes too old or dies. He takes the decisions for the community and his word is not queried. As befits the leader he lives in the best house and he and his family are highly respected. When Diane offered the salads to anyone who would do the washing up they were immediately offered without question to the headman's son who took them as of right.

This tribe being so near Georgetown is more sophisticated than those deep in the interior. They speak English and the old man told us as we were going round that the Arawak language was dying out in this tribe and it saddened him. He told me that if the children did not learn the language of their people they would lose respect for the Amerindian way of life. I do not remember ever having spoken to anyone with such a deep and unselfconscious sense of pride. The Amerindians are small and he was no exception, but he had a very weatherbeaten face and his walk and all his movements were naturally graceful. He did not smile to please us, he smiled when he thought something was amusing. He had worked on the timber grants most of his life and now he was too old.

The houses are all wooden and are beautifully kept. They are raised on stilts and alongside each house is an open room without walls, only a roof held up by poles and this is the kitchen. The village covers a large area and the houses are set in little groups of three or four and these groups were often a hundred and fifty yards or more apart. The women were mostly in their kitchens although some were in the houses attending to their children. Everyone said, "good afternoon" to us as we passed and if our guide asked them to show us something they were delighted to do so. In one house a woman was making a hammock out of a thick string which had been woven from palm leaves. She had almost finished it and it would not have looked out of place in any big London store. The small children were surprised to see us but they probably did not get too many visitors. Each house also had its own domestic scene with a large number of chickens running about.

Everyone wore European clothes and the missionaries have seen to it that most of the remote tribes now wear European dress although the Wai-Wai who live in the Essequibo and are the most natural tribe of all, still wear their tribal clothes. Santa Mission is only about fifty miles from Georgetown and when they are at home the younger ones go there quite often, but not apparently to buy anything. The old man said, "They go to look at the shops." There are certain things the Arawaks make which they sell for money, but they are themselves almost entirely self-sufficient, living off the land and killing animals and fish. In the three hours I spent going round the mission I saw hardly anything which had cost money. From the Ité palm leaves they make a kind of raffia and they use it among other things to make the seats of stools and a young girl by one house was making her stool on a frame interweaving green and purple raffia. The dye was one thing which had been bought.

They catch plenty of fish and hunt the swamps and forests for meat, killing mainly deer, labba, which is a big rodent about two feet long with sleek cinnamon hair, and otters. This tribe apparently hunted, mostly at night, with guns and torches, which must also have been bought. But until recently these Arawaks hunted with bows and arrows and blow-pipes and many of the tribes in the interior still do. They produce their own poison, curari, for the blow-pipes. It is a poison which produces paralysis in the heart muscles and the victims die of asphyxia because their lungs no longer work. Curari is used in open heart surgery.

The Arawaks at Santa Mission have some fields away from the mission where they grow cassava, plantains which they eat as vegetables, yams, sweet potatoes, tomatoes and star apples. The cassava is a rough skinned tuba rather like a yam and it has three uses. The cassava are grated and put in a Matape. A Matape is a long circular container made out of cane. It looks rather like a gigantic sausage and when it is empty it can be concertina-ed so that the grated cassava can be fed into its open end. When it is full it looks like a fatter and shorter sausage. The cane forms a loop at the top and when the Matape is full the loop is hung on a hook on a strong post. A large bowl is placed on the ground under it and a big stick is put through the wider loop at the bottom. Someone then sits on the stick and gradually the cassava is squeezed, the Matape goes back to its normal shape and all the juice runs out of the cassava into the bowl. The thick juice in the bowl is called Casareep and is boiled down until it becomes a dark, thick gravy with a strong flavour and it is used for stews. The Amerindians sell Casareep and it can be bought in London and anywhere where there is a big West Indian community.

When the grated cassava has been squeezed it leaves a residue which is dried over a fire until it looks like sugar grains and this is the staple diet of the Amerindians in most of tropical South America. It is dry and is mixed with water and flavouring, such as honey or gravy. If they want to make farine or flour from the residue they put it into a pan and stir until it coagulates. Then to make cassava bread the farine is put into a mortar and pounded into powder when it is put through a cane sieve and then it is mixed into a paste with water.

They make their own alcohol, Pawari, from the Cashew tree and they have Pawari feasts where this is drunk and it is reputed to be vicious. The Cashew tree has a pear-shaped fruit near the stem and a nut under the fruit. Pawari comes from the fruit which is boiled down with some herbs. It is said that after two glasses of Pawari, every time that person drinks water, for the next two days he gets drunk again.

The palm trees are another great source of raw materials. The houses are roofed by Ité palms. But the Ité palms cannot be cut until the "dark of the moon". If they are, a maggot matures inside and eventually eats everything away. Cynics have doubted this over the years and have invariably ended up without a roof over their heads. The Troolie palm fronds are used on the roofs as thatch. The bark of the Troolie palm is used to cover walls, the palm is cut and the bark is pounded and then taken off the trunk and stretched out and nailed on. There is almost nothing growing for which the Amerindians cannot find some use.

When we got back to our boat our picnic things had been washed up and put away, we said goodbye to the old man who shook our hands with great dignity and started back up the Kimune to the Demerara River, Atkinson Field, Georgetown and a cocktail party and the West Indies. But I had spent the day in South America. It was my final, incongruous glimpse of a part of the world which I found mostly beautiful, at times bewildering and always fascinating.

8

A job well done

This had been one of the most exciting Test series ever to have been played with four matches out of five going to the last half an hour. At Port of Spain in the First Test, Hall against all odds, held on with Sobers for 90 minutes to frustrate England. At Kingston, having all but won on the fourth day, England were scrambling to avoid defeat at the end of the 75 minutes on the extra sixth day. The Bridgetown Test was dull, but English nerves were glad of the rest. Then, back at Port of Spain Sobers made his declaration and England won with one over to go. And so to Gibbs' last agonising over at Georgetown.

Matches like these leave behind an unending flood of memories. There was the anxiety of the first morning of the series when Boycott and Edrich gave England a fine start. They were followed by Cowdrey's battle with Gibbs and then by Graveney's innings which for me remained the golden moment of the series. Then there was Lloyd's innings, that remarkable over before tea on the last day by Brown and finally Hall and Sobers. At Sabina Park, Sobers almost won the game single-handed after Snow had achieved the best figures of the series on a terrible wicket. There was also Cowdrey's century, Nurse's 74, the riots and the dramatic swing of fortunes afterwards.

Edrich's patience, an hour of Sobers and a gay innings by Lloyd on the last afternoon when the match was already drawn are the main memories from Bridgetown. The Fourth Test saw Kanhai at his best well-supported by Nurse and they were followed by Boycott and Cowdrey, and a delightfully cheeky innings by Knott. But all these were then submerged by Sobers's declaration and the batting of Boycott and Cowdrey which took England to victory. At Georgetown every quarter of an hour was a memory and on the last day, every ball; but Cowdrey, Knott and Sobers were the three most unforgettable performers in an amazing game of cricket.

There were the memories too of the lost opportunities. Hall's forward push which went over Boycott's head at forward short-leg on the last evening of the First Test. The catch D'Oliveira dropped at second slip at Sabina Park when Sobers was only seven in the second innings. Bridgetown was mercifully free from these incidents and so too was the Fourth Test until Sobers took it upon himself to declare. Soon afterwards Edrich pushed at Sobers and Murray dropped the catch. At Georgetown there were four occasions when England seemed safe only for disaster to follow. I remember most of all the look of sheer horror on Graveney's face when he glanced at Gibbs in the second innings and looked round in time to see the ball bounce up off Sobers's toe and Murray make a sudden lurch to his left when he saw his chance. The West Indians will remember the ball just before lunch when Knott cut at Gibbs and was dropped behind the wicket and the ball soon after lunch when Knott reached forward to Holford and snicked the ball slowly to Kanhai's right at slip. This catch also went down.

There could hardly have been a more eventful series and Titmus's accident in Barbados and Lock's arrival were two more pieces of drama. But there were other personal memories too. I remember so well the day's racing on the Savannah in Port of Spain, the 'Jump-Up' at the Portuguese Club and the Calypso Tents, the banana flambé at the Blue Mountain Inn and the 'Rock-Steady' in Jamaica, St. John's Church, the barber and the blacksmith's shop as well as the cold lunch at Paradise Beach in Barbados, the old woman brushing the outfield in St. Lucia, the Sparrow Spectacular in Georgetown and the most exciting day of all, going up the Kimuné to Santa Mission, and finally of course 'Mister Walker'. There is a lot to choose from.

Four such exciting finishes made this an unforgettable Test series, but it was a great series too. In almost every day's cricket some individual was stamping his own character on the game. There were none of those dull days where a side scores about 260 and no one gets more than 70 and each batsman looks alike. There were plenty of fine cricketers on both sides and in every match some of them were playing at their best. It requires great character to come back at the end of a long hot afternoon and faced with a seeming lost cause as Brown was at Port of Spain to muster the effort to bowl an over which takes three wickets. It needs character to bat as Sobers did at Sabina Park and at Georgetown and to bat as Knott and Cowdrey did in the same match and these are only five examples. Several of the big innings which were played were started at a time when the bowling side was on top and there is much more to an innings which shifts the balance of the game than one which simply consolidates an advantage already won.

The ultimate triumph of the tour was Cowdrey's. He answered his critics in the most convincing fashion. His performances with the bat gave him the foundation he needed, both for the side and for his own personal confidence. The chance of victory in the Fourth Test may have been handed to England, but in spite of the disappointments of the first two Tests and a tour which was by this time becoming hard work for some, Cowdrey had managed to maintain the enthusiasm in his side and when the chance came they were able to take it. He built up a strong team spirit and in his handling of critical situations particularly the riots at Kingston he showed that he has an instinct for diplomacy.

Some people criticised Cowdrey's minute to minute tactical handling of certain situations and when a captain is not successful, and England did not win either of the first two Tests having got into a strong position, he can always be criticised. But the unanswerable fact was that we won the series by one match and were very close to winning two more when three and a half months before, very few people were prepared to give Cowdrey even an outside chance of victory. Perhaps Close would have been lucky enough somehow to have winkled out those last two in the First Test Match, but would he have first led England to the situation where these two wickets were all they needed? In this series for the first time Cowdrey showed that the England captaincy was his by right although it had been acquired by default.

In the past Cowdrey has often been said to be too nice and too indecisive to make a good captain. He was as aware of these criticisms as anyone and was determined on this tour to disprove them. On the occasions he had captained England before he had been under a handicap as he was there either because someone was unfit or he was on trial. Now, for the first time it was his side and his responsibility. He is by nature a rather hesitant person but during the tour he seemed to become a tougher and more determined cricketer and at the same time he appeared to be more relaxed. This came from the confidence he was given by his own performances and the collective performances of the side as well as the knowledge that he had no one breathing down his neck. He saw that he could win and he was determined to do so. He injected this determination into the whole party and they raised their game accordingly, and he did not allow the frustrations and the noise and the drama which is cricket in the West Indies to affect the more solid temperaments of the Englishmen. It was a different and a wiser Colin Cowdrey who stepped into the aeroplane at Atkinson Field, Guyana on April 4th than the one who stepped out of the aeroplane at Seawell, Barbados on December 27th.

It was a satisfactory tour both in the result and for the future of English cricket. The three fast bowlers Snow, Brown and Jones who made up the biggest difference between the two sides arrived in the West Indies as fast bowlers with a lot of potential and they went home as seasoned and successful Test cricketers. An elbow injury has since ruled out Jones, but the others will be near the England side for some time. If any confirmation was needed Knott made it plain that he will be the England wicket-keeper for a long time to come. His batting in the last two Tests showed that it was a pity that the selectors did not have more confidence in him earlier. Pocock was quick to learn about bowling on hard wickets and the importance of length, line and flight and he will also be near the England side for a number of years.

Another reason England won the series was the consistent opening partnership of Edrich and Boycott. At the start of the series when most people were batting badly they gave England a fine start which took the pressure off the other batsmen and enabled them to build a total of 568 which gave the side's confidence an all-important boost. These two, like all good opening pairs, seem to complement each other at the wicket and it is a partnership which should continue for a long time.

Otherwise the bulk of the runs came from Cowdrey,

Barrington and Graveney. Apart from their centuries in the First Test Graveney and Barrington were not outstandingly successful, but they each played a bigger part in the overall success of the series than their figures suggest. Their advice was helpful to Cowdrey, Graveney fielded splendidly in the slips while Barrington got some useful wickets with his leg-breaks and also they both played important innings of around thirty and forty which were much more valuable than they look at first glance, and their experience was an important asset. The only member of the side who played in all five Tests without much success was D'Oliveira. His bowling kept him in the side, but he only took three wickets in the series and his use was purely defensive. There were times when he promised to make a big score, but his concentration often failed him when he had got over his customary bad start. It also failed him in the field for he dropped a surprising number of catches. Park's batting won him a place in three of the matches, but he never batted well during the whole tour. Ironically his wicket-keeping until he hurt his hand in the Third Test was as good as it has ever been. Titmus' tour was ended for him by the propellers of a speed boat although he had not been bowling well and there was a chance that he would in any case have lost his place to Pocock. His flight had been flat and he had not looked dangerous. The manager, L.E.G. Ames also played an important part in the success of the party and he and Cowdrey formed an excellent Kent partnership.

The West Indian atmosphere gives cricket a great deal of excitement and during these three and a half months the England side went through every emotion that the game of cricket can produce. But off the field too the West Indies is an exciting part of the world. The islands are physically different and the people are different. The girl who shouted "egas" in St. Lucia and the girl in the Cats Corner in Montego Bay who told me about Jamaica were worlds apart. The man who talked about Voodoo in the rum shop in Kingston could hardly have been more different from Gibbons in Barbados. In Guyana there are two completely different worlds less than half a day apart. Individuals can always be different, but these individuals were all typical of their own societies.

There will probably be riots at some future Test Match

somewhere in the West Indies. The majority of the West Indian people have had a slender education and are naturally excitable and immature. They get worked up and no one is going to prevent disappointment suddenly turning into resentment. Sophisticated European attitudes and standards which have been developed over many centuries should not be applied. The West Indians also have their gay, infectious enthusiasm which bubbles out so spontaneously. This is attractive; the riots are not, but in a sense they go together. There never have been and it is extremely unlikely that there ever will be riots at Lord's—anti-apartheid is something different—but so then it is just as unlikely that the English will ever produce a Sparrow Spectacular comparable to that night in Georgetown.

9

Across the Dateline

More than nine months later on December 15th eight West Indian cricketers stood on the pavement outside the Woolloongabba ground at Brisbane and, laughing, dancing, clapping their hands and moving their hips in time with the beat, they sang 'Mister Walker'. 'Good morning Mister Walker, ah come to see you daughter' and so on to the accompaniment only of themselves and the passing traffic. Although it was out of context it was a typical all-involving West Indian scene and the spontaneity of their joy and happiness was such that even with a few surprised Australians standing around rather solemnly and watching, it could hardly have been more natural. Barbados, Trinidad, Guyana and Jamaica were there living for a few moments through their emotions in their own islands; quite simply being themselves.

It turned out to be a poignant moment too, for it was the final hour of triumph for these West Indians who had in eight years seen so much success as well as doing a lot for the game of cricket. They had just beaten Australia by 125 runs in the First Test Match and they felt that night that the series was theirs for the taking. The strains of 'Mister Walker' rang out once again on the evening after the dramatic draw in the Fourth Test at Adelaide, but by then the overruling emotion for the West Indians was one of relief for having avoided defeat. They were already 2-1 down in the series and when three weeks later they lost the last Test Match they had in just over two months gone from carefree celebration to total despair. The West Indian temperament lives in the extremes, but this last extreme was sad because of its obvious finality.

That same evening at Brisbane the Australians slipped quietly away from the ground only too well aware of the opportunities they had thrown away in this match and as a result they collectively took away with them an even stronger determination to do better next time. This determination was seen in the next two months as they efficiently, systematically and completely destroyed the West Indians. Concentration, application and the desire to win gave their young side the singleness of purpose to break down the technical as well as the temperamental flaws of their opponents. By the end of the series the old West Indies side was unequivocally a thing of the past and the Australians who were lucky to draw the series in England six months earlier, were themselves approaching greatness. In the end they had not had too much against them, but they showed that they had all learned from their experiences in England and as a side had considerably widened the margin for error. They won the series deservedly and yet they never stood on the pavement and sang even 'Waltzing Matilda'.

Saturday in Australia is Friday in the West Indies and it seems appropriate that there should be a dateline between the two. The first most obvious difference between the two countries is their respective sizes. Australia is a vast land mass on the map somewhere near Asia, but size in that way means nothing. After five hours in an aeroplane between Perth and Brisbane and at the end of it the postage stamps are still the same it takes on a far more vivid meaning. It also takes a while to fly from Guyana to Jamaica, but here the stamps and the money are different and most of the journey is over the sea.

Because Australia is all the same country there are inside it obviously none of the physical and temperamental differences of the West Indian islands although the two countries themselves could hardly be more different. I spent a good deal of time in the five capital cities in the Southern half of the country, and although each one was in its own way different from the others they were mainly differences in outlook rather than innate differences of character. Years ago when ships reached Australia and put into Fremantle, people are said to have collected on the quayside and to have asked the passengers where they had come from. Adelaide was the next port of call and there the question was, "What religion do you belong to?" Onto Melbourne where it was, "What school were you at?" In Sydney, "How much money have you got?" and finally to Brisbane where the passengers were asked what they would like to drink.

Even now there seems to be something slightly appropriate in each of these questions. Perth is tucked away in a corner of Australia and because of the vast stretches of desert between there and Adelaide, it is the most isolated capital city in the world as well as being capital of Western Australia which was regarded for a long time as the Cinderella state. Adelaide, the only city not to come from convict origins, is a cathedral city with a relaxed and contented atmosphere and a gentle tempo of life. In the grassed Victoria Square in the centre of Adelaide there is a small avenue of trees which tries unsuccessfully to hide a tram station, a concession to progress, but beyond it a complicated and rather picturesque fountain glistens in the sun and there is a large and formidable statue of Queen Victoria.

Melbourne is a mixture of progress and reaction. Until three years ago the pubs shut at six in the evening although they now stay open until ten and Collins Street is the financial centre of Australia. There is a new and impressive art gallery which has been given over to the new and rising generation of Australian artists and a very English sector of society in South Yarra where "G.H." and "H.E." are often talked about in exaggerated stage whispers.

There is a natural antipathy between Melbourne and Sydney. New South Welshmen tend to regard Victorians as being too stuck up and pleased with themselves while the Victorians are apt to ride roughshod over the New South Welshmen. Sydney has felt a strong American influence. It was the only place in Australia where I was asked whether I meant Australian or US dollars. It has a thriving night club area, King's Cross, and all the sleaziness which goes with it as well as the beauties of Sydney Harbour, the Bridge, the remarkable unfinished Opera House and the more mundane but needful Martin Place where every building is big and solid and is either a bank or a post office. But I found Sydney the most egalitarian city in an egalitarian country.

A thousand miles further north and it is Brisbane and the sub-tropics. The humidity like the temperature is usually high and fierce tropical storms reverberate up and down the Brisbane river which gives the city its only real beauty. In some ways Brisbane seems to have been left behind for it is a city which does not have many of the amenities of a modern community. It has too a flavour of the East with the low wharves packed tight together along the edge of the river and it has an almost shanty-like atmosphere.

Every society in the world has its own conventions and idiosyncrasies and Australia is no exception. Some cities or groups of people were more hidebound by their own particular society, but everywhere I went I found in the Australians a natural, open friendliness. Australians are often said to be on the defensive with the English and "Pommy bastard" is an Australian phrase, but although I met a few who were only too eager to "knock" England, I got the impression that this reputation was more a hangover from the past when the English climbed aboard a ship at Tilbury and patronisingly visited Australia, looking down their noses most of the time. The Australians do not like people who give themselves airs and graces and this goes for other Australians as well as for visitors from abroad. If the Australians dislike someone for this or any other reason they say so. When I was in Kalgoorlie, the gold mining centre, I met a man of about fifty who was an executive for one of the mining companies and for a time we talked to another Australian who was the type who knew every answer there was. The next day watching cricket I ran into my executive friend and he began to talk disparagingly about this other man when suddenly I spotted him about two and a half paces away within earshot. I cautioned my friend who looked at me with a severe frown and said, "I don't care where he is" and continued talking about him in an even louder voice. There is a tough, pioneering streak in the Australians and this has given them a direct verbal approach which makes them call a spade a spade.

One of Australia's main disadvantages is that being originally populated by the English, it invites a closer comparison to England by the English than perhaps any other country. The English find a lot that is recognisable as stemming from England in terms of character and tradition, but then find that many of the details have in their eyes been distorted and in their eyes for the worse. But Australia is 12,000 miles from England and yet the different between the

English and the French who are only across the English
Channel are accepted. Maybe when people speak a different
language they are not expected to be the same and yet with
the vast distance, the environment, the climate and the size
of Australia it would be remarkable if the Australians and the
English were identical.

In real terms Australia is not much over a hundred years
old. The English brought their way of life with them but
soon they and their children became more and more divorced
from the society which produced this way of life. This meant
that Australians were being brought up with an inherited
tradition which did not entirely fit the mood or the need of a
fast-developing country. A hundred years is not long enough
for a tiny population in a vast continent to build its own
cultural and traditional base especially when for several years
their life was built round discovery and exploration and the
strongest instinct for many was for survival. They have
therefore developed the way of life that was given to them to
fit in with their needs and so while keeping the original base
they have adapted many of the details.

While individual character is difficult to find in the big
cities it is stronger and more readily accessible in the small
up-country towns. Mining and farming are two of the main
reasons for the development of these small communities. In
the towns I visited I found the people tough, straightforward
and self-sufficient and it was not for nothing that some of
their great-grandparents or grandparents even had set off into
the country with a water bottle strung round their backs not
knowing when it ran out where the next drink was coming
from. These townships have a strong identity of their own
and the people are proud of their own towns and there is an
innate self-confidence in their way of life.

It is an astonishing fact that in New South Wales alone
there are 126 provincial newspapers. Each one meets the
needs of a relatively small, isolated area which through sport,
business and social activities has a strong community spirit
and its own news is very important to it. This provincial
outlook carries through to the papers in each of the capital
cities which are at times surprisingly self-centred in their
search for news. It is obviously right that the people of any
city should want to read about the events that take place

within its boundaries and the cause and effect of economic, social and business influences within the area, but this is often done to the exclusion or at any rate to the extreme condension of important world news. *The Australian* which is printed in Canberra, Sydney and Melbourne is the only paper which attempts to be a national newspaper and to balance home and foreign news. It is also the only paper which sees its job as an interpreter as well as an informer for the other papers often tend to give the facts and not much more. Australian newspapers reflect the isolation of Australia and Australians both in terms of the outside world and within their own boundaries. They also reflect the size of the country and the needs of its minute population grouped here and there in varying sized parcels.

On the back or front pages of almost every paper I saw in Australia I was stopped by a large photograph of beautiful, blonde, bronzed, bikini-ed girls absorbing the sun or the surf at maybe Bondi Beach, Sydney, Brighton Beach, Melbourne, Rottnest Island off Perth, Glenelg in Adelaide or at Surfers Paradise, a holiday resort south of Brisbane. So much in the overall Australian way of life is moulded to their wonderful climate of which every possible advantage is taken. After turning past the sunbathing beauty one sooner or later comes to the large section of the paper which caters for sport. Australia is a country of sportsmen and I did not meet one person who was not passionately involved as a player or supporter in some aspect of sport. In their summer cricket, golf, tennis, racing and trotting are always catching the headlines and providing photographs while there is any amount of close season news about players involved in the various codes of football which the Australians play, Australian Rules Football, Rugby League, Rugby Union, Association Football, and Gaelic Football. At different times of the year swimming, surfing, baseball, squash, bowls, boxing, hockey, athletics, skiing and others have their turn.

I came back to Coogee the suburb in Sydney where I was staying during the Fifth Test Match when the driver asked me if I was interested in bicycle racing and went on to tell me that his son was well-known as a bicyclist in Australia and he brought a sheaf of cuttings out of the glove pocket about a series of races in Tasmania which his son had won. When we arrived at the flat where I was staying, I sat in the taxi for another five minutes while he told me about the intensive continuous training his son had to maintain. His father supervised this and each morning they would make a start soon after three o'clock. "I take my motor bike and he chases me. We use the roads going out of Sydney and there is not much about at that time. We do four hours then and he goes out again in the evening when he gets back from work."

There was another taxi driver in Sydney during the Fifth Test who had some harsh and weighty things to say about the cricket which was being played. When he stopped at a set of traffic lights he turned to the passenger sitting beside him who happened to be a recent Australian Test captain, "Did you ever play cricket?" he asked. "A bit, a long time ago," came the answer and the taxi driver continued to talk forcefully about the Australian side. Heroes are not remembered as they are in England. By then the West Indies were being badly beaten and by supporting them, the underdogs, he was revealing another Australian characteristic. In any hard fought contest between two sides the Australians are intensely patriotic, but once their opponents are being beaten easily and consistently a lot of Australians will want to see their fortunes change.

In such a vast country, and I only saw a small part of it, there is probably no such thing as a composite Australian character, but there are certain definite characteristics which I was able to pick up as much in isolated and insignificant conversations with taxi drivers or barbers or shop assistants, as at smart dinner parties. I learned as much from these meetings as from the other more dramatic things which I did. I spent an hour with a shift foreman 2,000 feet down a gold mine on Kalgoorlie's Golden Mile and in the Bush outside Kalgoorlie I watched an illegal gamblind game—Two-Up—in a makeshift corrugated iron casino. I was taken round the Mildura Winery in Victoria which produces some of the highest quality Australian wines. One evening in Brisbane I spent five hours in a police car which belonged to the drug squad and saw a remarkable side of life as well as eating about the best steak I ate while I was in Australia. I was taken on an evening cruise around Sydney Harbour, I spent a delightful week in Tasmania with its beautiful scenery and its strangely English countryside as well as spending fourteen hours in a sleeper between Perth and Kalgoorlie on a Sunday evening when alcohol cannot be bought, and I talked to a great many Australians wherever I went.

I arrived in Perth at two o'clock in the morning after spending nearly 27 hours in an aeroplane and the queue to immigration seemed longer and slower than most. The customs officer who looked at my bags several minutes later must have been near the end of his day too. He asked the usual questions in a rather flat voice and I told him that I had brought a thousand cigarettes with me and explained that I smoked Turkish cigarettes and that as I could only buy them in London I had brought enough with me to last for some time. He was very surprised and so I unpacked the ten boxes from my bag and he rather hesitantly picked one up and took the cellophane wrapping off and opened the lid. I assured him they were the cigarettes that I always smoked and that they were for myself, but he smelled them suspiciously, no doubt suspecting marijuana at the least, before calling over another customs man. They had a hurried whispered conversation before turning to me again and I suggested that they should both smoke one. I lit them both and after three or four draws the face of the man who had been dealing with me creased into a grin.

"I like them!" he said, "they're good. I'm going to finish this." And with that he marked my luggage and as I moved on he shouted after me, "Have a good time and don't smoke them too quick." He was grinning broadly. I was later told that the Perth customs were the most difficult in Australia.

Just before I reached Perth there had been several unpleasant earthquakes in the area and one village—between Perth and Kalgoorlie had been completely destroyed and some of the tremors had been felt in Perth. I was taken from the airport to my hotel about twenty-five minutes away by a small rotund middle-aged taxi driver and we soon began to talk about these earthquakes. As it happened he lived in the area which had felt one, but he also remembered another from a long time ago and was unmoved by the present series. I asked him how badly his own house had been affected.

"Nothing," he said, "We were in bed and suddenly the

ceiling began to move and the pictures jumped about. My wife was hysterical and she jumped out of bed and ran screaming into the garden, but I saw at once what was happening and it wasn't a bad one so I stayed where I was and it soon stopped."

When I arrived at my hotel I found that the night porter was a newly arrived Italian emigré who spoke very little English. I repeated my name nearly a dozen times and spelt it about as often. He kept on looking up at me and then back at the desk and shaking his head. He said something and disappeared through some swing doors and returned five minutes later looking no more hopeful. Eventually he decided that although he had never heard of me before there was an empty room I could have. The next morning I discovered that my name had been spelt "Blofell" in the list of people staying.

These three incidents were all in their own ways part of Australia. By talking openly and straight to the customs officer unlike two Englishmen near me who were going through an embarrassing "these small-minded customs people" routine, the whole operation was quicker, more friendly and straightforward. The taxi driver like most Australian men was an obvious male supremacist and the earthquake would not have worried him very much, but, well, women are women and in Australia they are the lesser of two equals. Finally the Italian emigré or New Australian was the first of many Europeans in Australia who drive taxis—it was possible to go for three or four days without coming across an Australian taxi driver, work in hotels, wait in restaurants and other similar jobs; some speak English well while many of them have trouble in forcing it through their guttural wheezing. It will be interesting to see how much these Europeans contribute to the development, particularly the cultural development of Australia as they come from imaginative races and they seem bound to play an important part in the future shape of their new country.

Perth itself is an island within an island. It is 2,000 miles from Adelaide across the Nullarbor Plain, and is nearer to Singapore than to Sydney and also it is capital of the state which wanted to remain outside the Federation of Australian states. As a result, it has a strong spirit of insularity, but no more of inferior insularity. It is at the moment going through a fast moving and exciting period of change both physically and in the mental attitude of its people. Western Australia is by far the largest of the Australian states being more than ten times bigger than the United Kingdom, but its population numbers only 850,000. Being so big and so much of it so arid and inaccessible, little money has come to Western Australia for the purpose of developing it. But now the rich mineral deposits in the state which are in terms of size only just beginning to be tapped, the fertile lands in the South and the coming of industry and tourism to Perth has given the people an exciting prospect for the future and prosperity which have in turn helped to give them their self-respect which has put them on a level with the people of the other cities. When I was in Perth I found a general feeling of optimism and confidence and the people talked about "the East" in a much less derogatory sense than maybe was once the case.

The city of Perth is a mixture of a distant colonial outpost, gleaming steel girders and skyscrapers and comfortable surburban living. Modern office blocks and motels which have become a symbol of modern life in Australia, are taking over the skyline from the solid old colonial hotels and the rows of shops with wooden canopies stretching out over the pavements, the age of which is disguised neither by the bright advertisements nor new coats of paint. Big new contemporary shopping centres are appearing and along the skyline looking at Perth from across the Swan River where the suburbs stretch away for ever, are several tall palm trees looking out of place among the noise and speed of the urban life, but nonetheless standing triumphantly in their own way and they introduce another ingredient which helps give Perth its own special flavour.

Visually Perth is brought to life by the Swan River and King's Park. The mouth of the Swan is a few miles away in Fremantle and when the river reaches Perth it balloons out beyond the Nanows Bridge into a thousand acre basin which is known as Perth Water. King's Park with its fine flowers and shrubs and trees stands high up behind Perth Water and gives it a handsome background especially in the evening sun. It is remarkable then to find such a wide combination of colours being so truly reflected by the dark water.

King's Park is not quite high enough up or far enough away for the whole view to be taken in at one glance. One looks straight down from the Park onto Perth Water. The city opens out to the left and across the other side colourful suburbia with red roofs sticking out of a mass of green foliage stretches away for ever. It is one of those satisfying views where the longer one looks the more detail appears.

A high proportion of the Australian population lives in the big towns and cities and in their splendid climate a vast and very comfortable suburban society has grown up with all the conformity that this suggests. In all the big cities the suburban bungalows stretch for miles with their carefully kept and brightly coloured gardens and their ever-working sprinklers. Walking through a suburb at the weekend there is hardly a garden which is not being respectfully attended to or a car that is not being polished or washed. This way of life suits the Australians and in the climate is obviously infinitely preferable to living right among the bricks and mortar and constant dust of the city centre. The result of this is that the main off-duty activities of the population take place around the perimeter of the cities and the city centres except Sydney offer no great attraction or pull like for example Piccadilly at a weekend. Living in this way the Australians are extremely contented: they like an ordered life in pleasant surroundings. So often the term suburbia sounds patronisingly mundane, but in Australia it is the basis of a universal way of life which has grown up with the country and suits it.

Somewhere between Perth and Adelaide watches have to be put forward by an hour and a half, but once on the ground it seems that they should have been moved almost a generation the other way. Adelaide is a city of stately elegance and tranquillity which comes from a combination of its imposing array of stone buildings in the centre, its physical setting with the comfortable suburbs stretching sleepily up to the surrounding foothills and the unhurried way of life. It is a city where nothing goes very fast except the taxis and its society is one of the most friendly in the country.

It is a conventional society too with the people living and moving almost exclusively around among their own particular groups or cliques with the Adelaide Club claiming nearly all the influential men in the city. Industry and the changes it brings has crept into Adelaide but barely perceptibly and driving out of the city into the Barossa Valley, which produces many good wines, the road passes a huge abbattoir with cattle in the holding yards sadly awaiting their turn. There is a strong putrid smell which takes several miles to get out of the car and it is a reminder although a slightly unpleasant one that the land has brought the area much of its wealth.

Adelaide is the most relaxed and peaceful of the Australian cities I visited and yet it has about it a musty flavour of the past. The city centre laid out with all the neat precision of a geometry box with the streets running North to South and East to West in exact rectangles, is filled with stately Victorian buildings made from the local freestone. They make an appropriate backcloth to the statue of Queen Victoria, but the people themselves have none of this reserve.

It is a city where people tend to live and mix only in their own groups, but they are relaxed with it. Their society may instinctively maintain its inherited protocol and class base, but I found it pleasantly unselfconscious about it all and as far as I was concerned nothing was too much of an effort to see that I had what I wanted. Without the business and wealth of Sydney and Melbourne or the expanding horizons of Perth, Adelaide is content with itself and has more of a small-town atmosphere. But it is a city which gave the impression that it has what it wanted and is happy to hang onto it rather than have wild ambitions for the future.

From this small city centre the suburbs stretch lazily away to the foothills of the Mount Lofty Ranges. Of course Adelaide has changed in recent years as industry and commerce with all the trimmings have tentatively explored the city. There are the inevitable tall new office blocks looking like so many glass match boxes piled on top of each other, but somehow the calm of this cathedral city remains The aeroplanes circling overhead leave behind a roar that is intrudingly harsh and the pneumatic drills clatter that much more distastefully.

There are many squares and pieces of parkland which fill Adelaide with open spaces and sunlight. The formality of the northern part of King William Street with its banks and post offices and the city hall is broken in the time it takes to cross a road, North Terrace. It runs across King William Street and on the far side of it rich green parkland with the Torrens River flowing through and the Botanical Gardens across to the right, provide a glorious contrast framed in the far distance by the hills. The Torrens Lake which is artificially built looks at first like a big river, but the river itself is a little more than a trickle and it has been dammed to create the lake.

Adelaide is short of good restaurants, but one of the best, Ernest's, is on the banks of the lake. I dined there on a glorious evening and the glow of the city lights as they were reflected out of the water more than made up for the tables which were crammed too close together. The wines in Adelaide were good, many of them coming from the nearby Barossa Valley, but the best wine I drank like the best food I ate was given to me in private houses. The motels, as they did everywhere, produced a diet which was based on oysters or prawn cocktails and steaks or fish and there was nothing very imaginative about the cooking. There are not many ways of cooking a steak, but some good sauces would have been a help.

It was in Adelaide that I was first introduced to Oysters Kilpatrick which I found much the best way of eating the Australian rock oysters. The oysters cooked with small pieces of bacon and Worcester sauce and later some French mustard helped. By the time all this had happened to them they were no longer oysters, but the combination produced a good taste. I was rather disappointed by the Australian oysters, but maybe this was bound to happen as I am a passionate lover of the English mud oysters. The rock oysters are very small with nowhere near the fulsome taste of the larger mud oysters. In Australia natural oysters, and most restaurants have two or three different ways of cooking them as well, are always served with a small pot of tomato sauce in the middle of the dish.

There are not too many alternatives in Adelaide when it comes to spending a night "on the town". I went several times to the Arkaba Hotel which combines the luxuries of high class living accommodation with a variety of bars and restaurants. It is the centre of Adelaide night life and the biggest of the restaurants has a large dance-floor and a cabaret—of Fijian dancers when I was there. In the evenings the Arkaba is a great meeting place and although the restaurant was expensive—an evening for two with wine could cost around fourteen dollars or seven pounds—it was usually full. Ideally the big restaurant was rather impersonal with the problems of slow service which bedevilled almost every restaurant in Australia, but the twisting bars downstairs had plenty of atmosphere. The Arkaba fulfilled a need, but in time other places which offer the same in a slightly different way will spring up and probably take over.

The two night clubs I tried to go to were tucked away in narrow streets, at least in places which the bulk of the New Australian taxi drivers did not know, and both of them were more or less deserted. I never discovered whether this was a reflection on my choice of club, my time of arrival or just that the darker night spots have not yet caught on. The most amusing and interesting evenings I spent in Adelaide were in private houses and a lot of the entertaining is done at home. This may help explain the shortage of evening entertainment in Adelaide.

One evening in Adelaide I was taken to a drink party where I knew no one and yet when I left an hour and a half later I had received no less than five invitations to go out to dinner the following night. I turned down four and took down the address of the fifth which was in the foothills. The next evening I arrived rather late having spent a considerable time trying to convince my taxi driver that my way was better than his. When I was inside a very picturesque bungalow type house built in the side of the hill my host gave me some whisky. I drank water with it and he told me that when he was last in England, he had been staying in Birmingham and one evening had ordered a whisky and soda. After a long wait he received a concoction which had a terrifying taste and it turned out that the English waiter had been confused by the Australian accent and had brought along a whisky and cyder. I myself found the Australian accent easy to understand. Whole syllables are swallowed and it has a healthy twang, but it was very seldom that I failed to pick up a word. All visitors to Australia at some stage get hold of *Lets talk Strine* which deals phonetically with the Australian language. It professes to be written by Professor Aufferbeck Lauder (alphabetical order) and it goes from there stressing, among other things, the importance of "aorta" which although it has the answer to everything as I discovered, has nothing to do with the heart, but simply "they ought to". Aorta build a new road, aorta pass a new law and so on.

I got my whisky and this developed into one of the most interesting evenings I spent in Australia. There were six of us and for a long time we talked about the strengths and weaknesses of Australia and the Australian character. I did not often find the Australians prepared or able to talk objectively about themselves and although no startling revelations were made it was interesting to hear from an Australian about the attitudes and prejudices of the older generations which inevitably had coloured their thinking and had left its mark in their children. Australia is such an easy country to live in that when discussing it in the comfort of a modern house in Adelaide it is easy to forget the difficulties and hardships that were ever-present a hundred years ago and the mark they must have left on the national character. Before I went my host mentioned a book about Australia which he had enjoyed and found reasonably accurate. I began to write down the title when he went into the next room and came back with a copy, his only copy, which he gave to me and I still have.

Adelaide accepts tradition without being hidebound by it. The people will face the future when they have to, but just now they are happy with what they already have. The old stone buildings and the skyscrapers fit in side by side and new ideas and moods are tempered by this tradition. One day maybe the new will take over, but it will not be just yet.

The rivalry between Melbourne and Sydney is strong yet sometimes laughable. Melbourne may be fifty years younger than Sydney, but it is a quieter, more sedate city. There is a conservative atmosphere about Melbourne, an atmosphere one might find in parts of England, but one which is strangely out of place in this environment. It makes the city appear to be taking itself too seriously as if it is disapproving or perhaps jealous of the freer and more cosmopolitan life in Sydney. I listened on countless occasions to verbal exchanges, some playful, some not so playful, between Victorians and other Australians, usually New South Welshmen.

I had only been in Perth for a week when after dinner one evening the argument began. It built up to a fair intensity and although both combatants were very cheerful one felt that deep down they were being serious. The argument introduced me to several of the delightful no-nonsense Australian expressions. The Victorian had listened to his attacker with resigned disbelief on his face. When his opponent had finished he leant forward in his chair. "Pig's ear to that" and the tone was hardly flattering. To stick to roughly the same metaphor, "Pig's ear" or "Pig's arse" means "My foot".

The most charming twist to this rivalry between the two biggest cities happened on my first visit to Melbourne. The Victorians regard the MCG as the greatest cricket ground in the world and in a sense they are right for it holds 120,000 after being enlarged for the 1956 Olympics, but with all its concrete it has little atmosphere. The Sydney Cricket Ground with the Hill and Botany Bay in the far distance from high in the Noble Stand has far more character. I was being driven one morning to the MCG by a friend who was also a member when he asked me to hold onto his metal membership badge. I read the inscription on the front and then I turned it over and was amused to see printed in small letters right at the bottom "made in Sydney".

The centre of Melbourne is the most dignified and businesslike of all the city centres and Collins Street, itself the financial centre of Australia stretches through the middle. The solid old buildings now looking like so many Victorian ladies are gradually being edged out by tall modern office blocks with lifts which race up twenty floors in less time than it takes to blow one's nose and without leaving one's tummy in the basement either. At lunchtime the pavements are full of bronzed and beautiful girls with colourful mini-skirts which grow unashamedly higher and higher—maybe in the heat they need to. The mini-skirts, the skyscrapers, the bustle on the pavements, the rushed authority of high-powered business men racing across to a taxi, late for their next appointment and finishing their last one over their shoulders as they go, and the cosmopolitan flavour of the Southern Cross Hotel all give Melbourne a challenging and competitive aura. It is, however, the formal aura of the City of London rather than the more casual, happy-go-lucky approach of the Americanised Sydney. It is appropriate that the centre of Melbourne is looked down upon by the enormous white turreted wedding cake that is Government House. It helps lend the city a certain regal stiffness which it wears easily.

It is a city where the English way of life has been followed in closer detail than elsewhere and the Victorians have inherited some of the Englishman's love of tradition. The rich send their sons to Geelong, the Australian equivalent of Eton and life follows a more rigid pattern there. I found too that many of the people I met in Melbourne were initially more reserved than the Australians in the other cities. The women are dressy while their men are for the most part very conservatively dressed. The younger generation seem wild and permissive with their pleasures but in a rational way, and without going to extremes with their clothes or to drugs for an extra kick out of life. It will be a long time before the Australian character succumbs completely to Carnaby Street. It was no coincidence that Melbourne spurned Jean Shrimpton when she appeared at Flemington for the Melbourne Cup, in its way as big an occasion as Royal Ascot, wearing a mini-mini-skirt before they had become accepted.

The sprawling suburbs of Melbourne cover a large area. First, on the south bank of the River Yarra within ten minutes drive of Collins Street there is South Yarra and Toorak, the Melbourne equivalents of London, SW1 and SW3 sliced in two by the long Toorak Road, the Sloane Street if not the King's Road with its dress shops, butchers' shops that everyone knows, restaurants from delightful bistros to Maxim's with St. John's Church looking squarely down on most of its length.

It is socially "right" to live on the South Bank of the Yarra and these two suburbs house most of the city's influential people. Architecturally the suburbs are a mixture. In the more prosperous areas there are peaceful old Victorian houses set back from the pavements with high walls enclosing their gardens, but sadly these older houses are constantly being pulled down to make way for blocks of flats. And set in amongst them are many pleasant modern bungalow houses designed to make the most of the climate and at the same time afford protection against it when necessary. They are spaciously laid out with attractive gardens and the ever-essential swimming pool lurking somewhere. The gardens are a glorious patchwork of colours: poinettias, bougain-villeas, hibiscus, many kinds of roses and flowering shrubs and the owners usually as hospitable as anyone one could want to meet.

From South Yarra the suburbs fall away in a descending scale of excellence with the houses becoming duller and more drab. They are anyway uninspiring being a compromise between the old and the new. The poorer suburbs which are several stations out on the network of suburban railway lines house many of the European emigres and in the big new supermarkets which serve these areas Australian is spoken with many curious accents. The low houses which line the streets in these areas have not been well cared for. The brickwork and the masonry are usually chipped; the paint has flaked off the windows and the gardens are often overgrown. The people living here are waiting for the chance to move.

Architecturally the old Colonial suburban houses are much the most interesting. Built towards the end of the last century they are unmistakeable with their broad verandas and their intricately patterned panoplies of iron lacework around the balconies and the verandas. There are some squares in South Melbourne almost perfectly preserved and each individual house is a study on its own with its own peculiarities. There are some similarly ornate streets of terraced houses in Paddington in Sydney. Unfortunately, a vast number of these old houses have made way for progress of one sort or another—progress built with modern materials.

As a city, Melbourne has a lot to offer visitors, but one of the "musts" is the new Art Centre with its own fascinating design and its contents which are the work of the new generation of Australian artists.

I enjoyed every moment in Melbourne and the hospitality I was given was superb. The third day I was there I went to a

Hunt Ball out by Essendon Airport where some of the men wore pink coats and the party could easily have fitted into an English stately home. I went to more good and different restaurants in Melbourne than in any other city, Fanny's, Maxim's, Lazar's, The Two Faces, Bernardis and so on. I was taken to an auction sale where heavy old-fashioned bedroom furniture fetched prodigous prices and old prints were like gold dust. I found a shop in the Arcade around the Southern Cross Hotel which sold Balkan Sobranies. It was in Melbourne that I learned to drink Australian style, for they do not call a halt between lunch and six o'clock and in the heat, gin and tonics were undoubtedly an asset in mid-afternoon. I visited a number of exceptional houses in South Yarra and Toorak and there was often a bottle of Great Western Champagne in the fridge and I met many charming and interesting people besides. I can understand why the Victorian said, "Pig's ear" to his friend from Sydney.

But I can also understand why the New South Welshman might have said, "Pig's arse" to the Victorian when his turn came. Sydney is a frenetic, impulsive city which gives off a certain animal magnetism. It is brash and slightly arrogant and yet almost every Australian I met soon asked, "Have you been to Sydney?" Then, almost before I had given my answer, they would tell me what they thought of it. I met no one who was indifferent to Sydney. Either it was dirty and dishonest or else it was next door to heaven. I came away from Sydney with several impressions, the main one being that it was the most un-Australian place I visited in Australia. Sydney is as untypical of Australia as New York is of the United States of America. I did not find Australia a brash country.

Sydney is the most free and exciting of the Australian cities. It is set out with none of the precision of the others. Wide and narrow streets run haphazardly into each other for ever climbing or descending one of the many small hills on which Sydney is built. The bustle on the pavements, the people pouring into pubs and milk bars, the traffic blocks, the angry blare of horns, the colourful newspaper stalls in Martin Place, a short stubby street which is the city centre, the milling throngs in the small parks, the rushing taxis which never seem to be empty, and always about to knock someone down, the Expresso Bars, the dirt on the pavements and the old newspapers lying at the side of the road: all give the impression that life is going twenty miles an hour faster than it actually is.

Sydney was founded in 1788 because of its fine natural harbour and it is the harbour which still gives Sydney its fame as well as its beauty. There cannot be many more exciting waterways in the world. The Harbour is a vast complex of bays and peninsulas and there is not a dull view to be seen through the many miles of winding coastline. There could be no Sydney without the sea. The ships dock almost in the city centre at Circular Quay which stands at the end of Pitt Street. Sydney Harbour Bridge and the Opera House are both wonders of the modern world. The Bridge is the longest single arch bridge in the world and is wonderfully impressive in the way of all unbelievable architectural feats. From far away its skeleton appearance makes it look as if it were made from a child's Meccano set, but it is a staggering construction.

The Opera House is built out into the bay like some gigantic pre-historic monster reincarnated in concrete and steel. The Opera House is still unfinished for the costs have soared to nearly ten times the original £4 million estimate, but the shell itself is there. The huge white sails of the roof rise up from the water's edge like enormous ears which dwarf even the Harbour Bridge. It is a vast and incredible concept which when and if it is finished will have several opera halls, a theatre, dressing rooms and all the amenities that are essential, but they will be in luxurious form.

The sea also provides the most popular form of relaxation in Sydney. There are miles and miles of glorious beaches where the Sydneysiders worship the sun, the surf and the sand. Take Bondi Beach at a weekend. It is almost impossible to see a square inch of sand let alone to find a patch big enough to sit down on. The sea is full of bobbing, crawling, shouting heads and the surf riders streak for shore like so many crossing curves on the same piece of graph paper. Ice-cold drinks are being swallowed feverishly by the colourful multitude, the cans up to the lips. The girls have baked their skins into a dark mahogany brown and their gay bikinis are protecting decency in the briefest possible way while the men lope their way to the water's edge looking like the healthy young Australian males they are, each an advertisement for a physical fitness course. Bondi is a spreading semi-circle of beach around one of Sydney's many bays situated almost in the middle of Sydney. The buildings look down on this scene almost as if they belong to another world. There are quieter and more attractive beaches than Bondi, but this stretch of sand means Sydney to the rest of the world as much as the Bridge and the Opera House.

Sydney's cosmopolitan flavour comes into focus in King's Cross. The flickering electric signs, the casual clothes, the American accent, the strong smell of food coming from the steak bars, the groups of men standing around the entrance of the clubs, the gurgle of canned music coming out of everywhere that is selling anything, the shouts from within the pubs, the mass of people and the litter underfoot are all part of the compulsive lure of a vibrant night club area. The signs flicker, The Whisky Agogo, The Pink Pussy Cat and so on. The doormen look closely at each customer as he enters and there is a continual trickle down the stairs to the dark sin beyond. When I was in King's Cross almost every other man I saw was an American soldier on R and R (rest and recuperation) from Vietnam. They wanted a good time and were going to find it. Then there were the tourists who had come from other parts of Australia joyfully determined to take back home vivid reports of Sydney's attractions. There were overseas visitors, some having a holiday, others working who had taken the night off to "unwind". And all the time the tills were eating up the dollar bills.

Like the other Australian cities, Sydney has its own mass of suburbs. I stayed in Coogee out from the centre of Sydney past the race course at Randwick and it took me time to get over the contrast between the tempo of the city centre and pace of Coogee which is on the sea with an attractive bay and a fine beach. Coogee was like a small town on its own. The main shopping street had everything a housewife could possibly need and after I had been to the dry cleaners a few times and done some shopping for the people I was staying with, the shopkeepers knew who I was and were always anxious to talk. Coogee had a marvellously friendly atmosphere and the people there were very quick to accept me. No one was stilted or reserved and everyone was each other's friend. There were no false airs and graces about most of Sydney and its people.

Parts of the centre of the city are attractive. The gardens along the side of Macquarie Street offer a refreshing array of greenery. Being built on a series of hills—Sydney is a city of many levels and therefore exciting views. Several times walking through the city I came to a flight of stairs cut through the sandstone to connect different levels. One of the best views of the Harbour is looking across from Rushcutter Bay which is just below King's Cross. The drive around the cliffs of the Harbour puts all its many intricacies into yet another new and exciting perspective. The road passes Fisherman's Lodge a fish restaurant and the best of any at which I ate in Sydney. It was all sea food, the cooking was good and the menu as imaginative as sea food allows.

Paddington is one of the oldest parts of Sydney and it is the most charming of all the many suburbs I saw in Australia. The tiny Victorian terraced houses standing in narrow winding streets have been taken over by the intellectuals. These houses with their iron balconies and lacework have been carefully renovated and gaily painted. It all makes a nicely gentle Bohemian atmosphere for the rising generation of Sydney artists.

On the surface Sydney may seem brash and money-conscious, but there is a lot in the sprawling acres of this, the biggest of the Australian cities, to find and unravel. In a month I could hardly scratch the surface, but I saw enough I think to realise the possibilities.

The sun shines almost unceasingly in Australia and for an English visitor maybe this is the first and greatest miracle. Perth in October, Adelaide and Melbourne in November had all however been attacked by cold winds and although the sun shone it did not provide much warmth. In Sydney in late November it was hot, but Brisbane was sub-tropical. The humidity was uncomfortably high and by the time I had walked across the tarmac to the Airport building with a briefcase and a typewriter I was dripping wet.

Queensland's coastline runs for more than 3,000 miles up to the Gulf of Carpentaria in the North of Australia. Brisbane, the capital of the state is situated in the south near the New South Wales border and it has a character to suit its way of life, which does not necessarily fit the sizeable but remote towns in the other parts of the state.

Brisbane is given physical character by its river which gives the city its name. This large waterway twists and turns below Brisbane's bridges nearly twenty miles upstream from Moreton Bay. My hotel looked down on it from high on the north bank and each morning the boats came slowly up the river causing a ripple which on this wide stretch of water had almost disappeared before reaching the shore. I never discovered what the boats were carrying. Some used to tie up at the low tightly packed wharfs a little way upstream on the other side; other chugged on out of sight under the steel girders of one of Brisbane's six bridges and on round to the right. Each morning I used to go into the city by way of the little ferry which started from just outside the hotel. It took five minutes to cross the river and cost threepence, chug, chug on uncomfortable wooden seats in a boat called *Susan*, and it made a charming start to the day.

Brisbane is essentially only a country town. After Sydney life hardly seems to move. It has some of the old-world formality which is so strong in the up-country towns; it is content to be parochial while architecturally apart from its handsome town hall with its fluted Ionic columns; it is the same part-anonymous, part-incongruous mixture of young and old. In Brisbane's case the old is rather shabbier than in the other cities probably because the buildings were originally put up to serve a country town and not a capital city. There are new stores and office blocks in the middle of Brisbane, but it is a city centre without much character. In spite of the shabbiness of some of the houses and streets, Brisbane has plenty of open parkland within its boundaries. The greatest blessing however to have been bestowed on Brisbane in modern times is air conditioning. With the high humidity when I was there life without air conditioning would have been intolerable. There are some pleasant new motels in Brisbane which are gradually eclipsing the old Victorian palace of Lennons Hotel. It summed up Brisbane that one of the most popular places in the evenings was the vast dining room/restaurant in Lennons where after a long cabaret, dancing was conducted to the strains of a big and rather formidable band. There was also the "Playboy Club" which had nothing at all to do with Hugh Heffner, the prices were high, the comforts slender, but with no alternatives they could afford to be.

One evening during the First Test Match I was having a shower before dinner when the telephone rang and Keith Butler who writes for the *Adelaide Advertiser* asked me to go up to his room to meet some friends. When I got there I was introduced to the head detective of the Queensland drug squad, and his two offsiders, the number two with him in his car and the driver. Keith knew Jack and asked him back to have a drink when he met him at the cricket. He had just come back from the North of the state where he had been involved in a big case of growing and selling marijuana. In North Queensland the drug grows like weeds and the police have to try and prevent it from finding its way down to King's Cross and any other markets there may be. It had taken them as far North as Bowen which produces the finest

mangos in the world. He had a box in the boot of his car and sent one of his men to get some for Keith and myself. They were so juicy that once I had taken the skin off I should have stood naked in the bath to eat them, but they were quite unforgettable and better than the mangos I ate in the West Indies. He gave me four and they made four of the stickiest, but the best breakfasts I shall eat for some time.

After a while Jack looked at his watch and said that they ought to go as they were on duty, but would Keith and I like to come round in the car with him. Of course we jumped at the idea and I changed into a suit to look more the part, but without the homburg hats they wore I felt I was easily distinguishable as an amateur. Our guide has a great reputation in Queensland and had won medals for his bravery. For some years he served in the Gulf of Carpentaria which is one of the toughest places in Australia and as we went around Brisbane that evening there was no doubting the respect for Jack, a tough leathery little man in his forties, from both good and bad alike. He had too a quick, good sense of humour, although he was a man of fairly few words.

He had promised us that he would see we got the best piece of meat in Australia for dinner that night. Having signed on again over the walkie-talkie when we got into the car and found that he was not wanted anywhere, we headed for Breakfast Creek Inn, a Creek. which comes off the Brisbane River. It was crowded but a table was soon produced for the five of us and after choosing our own uncooked steaks we drank some beer and waited. The steak which came for me was vast and it was probably the best piece of meat I ate in over four months in Australia, anyway one of the most remarkable. When we had finished we were soon back in the car and having again signed on with the police station Jack decided where to go.

He asked me if I had noticed many Aborigines in Brisbane and I said that I had not. He smiled and told me that I would have done if I had known where to look. In about ten minutes we stopped outside an enormous ramshackle pub and with Jack and his two offsiders going first, Keith and I followed on behind. The room was full of Aborigines. Inside we went straight up to the bar, but the conversation which amongst about three hundred people was loud, had suddenly stopped. Everyone was looking round at Jack and the rest of us. He had a hurried conversation with the pub keeper, asking him whether he had seen certain people and then we sat down round a table to drink our beer. By now the conversation was only very desultory and most eyes were still on us. We were talking quietly when suddenly Jack noticed something; he leant quickly across in his chair and asked a hurried question to one of the others who brought out his wallet. He pulled out a photograph which Jack looked at and nodded. He spoke again very briefly and the other two got up and started to thread their way to the far end of the room. "There's someone over there we want," Jack said to us, "if there's any trouble go and stand by the door." Jack sat still deliberately not watching and soon they came back with an Aborigine girl in her twenties. She was frightened, "We're not going to hurt you," Jack assured her and we all got into the car, the girl between Jack and the driver. On the way to the station Jack asked the girl if she was in trouble again and she replied that she had only been let out of prison the day before. She asked what the police wanted her for and was told that they wanted to ask some questions and if she was a good girl and told the truth nothing would happen to her. When we got to the station the driver took Keith and myself to Jack's room and the other two took the girl away. In Jack's office there were many marijuana plants which he had brought south from his last case. We looked at photographs of the plants growing wild and without care which showed the size of their problem and there were some horrifying photographs of some hardened addicts.

It was not long before we were back in the car again and with the time nearing ten we did a tour of some of the other disreputable drinking places. We arrived in one at three minutes to ten and within forty-five seconds of us appearing the place was empty; again almost all the people were Aborigines, many of whom were mixed up with crime of some sort. We went to one or two other places where there might have been trouble and it was amusing to watch some of the toughies we met who literally wilted at the sight of Jack. One of the two men with him told me during the evening that he was the toughest but the fairest of all the police up there. Once ten o'clock was past we cruised around for more than an hour checking up on various dives before the car pulled up outside a pub which the police knew well and sold them beer in the "inner" room when they wanted. Soon after we arrived the doors opened and in came Ray Lindwall, and the conversation ranged from drugs to cricket, to Sydney and back to the present Test Match. As we stood round the bar one of the policemen half made as if to take off his jacket and underneath I saw the strap and the black bulge of a shoulder holster. The drug squad in Queensland have some pretty tough assignments and if a body of men deserve this sort of protection, it is them. It was getting on for one o'clock when Jack and his henchmen dropped us back at our motel, leaving me with four Bowen mangos, the memory of a remarkable evening which showed me part of Brisbane which left to myself I could never have seen, and an uncomfortable feeling that I must have missed a lot on my way round Australia to Brisbane.

To riches by sleeper

Kalgoorlie, 350 miles North-East of Perth, is probably the most famous of the Australian gold mining towns. Gold now comes out from as far as 3,000 feet below ground in an only marginally profitable trickle, but the big new nickel "finds" in the area are bringing the people and the town of Kalgoorlie back to life. It is the only town in Australia where there are still legalised brothels. It is a far cry from there to Murgon, a small agricultural town about 120 miles North-West of Brisbane. Cattle, potatoes, peanuts and wheat provide the town with its prosperity. The cricket ground where the West Indians played a South Queensland Country Eleven is the local showground which is also the rodeo centre.

Mildura in the North of Victoria on the South Australia border exists only because of the irrigation which is provided by the Murray River. It has become one of the main centres of the Australian Wine Industry and well-known Australian wines like Coonawarra Claret are produced in this area, and the working men's club has the longest bar in the world.

There is a great contrast between these three towns and the atmosphere, the geography and the climate of Tasmania. Kalgoorlie originally belonged to a period earlier this century when gold was very profitable, but has been jerked back into the present by the nickel, while Murgon and Mildura are towns with a more contemporary atmosphere which seems to beckon to the future. Tasmania is an island which belongs more closely to the past. The sense of history is stronger than anywhere else I found in Australia, life moves at a more gentle tempo and is altogether less urgent than on the mainland. Tasmania is growing and developing, but it is blending progress with what it already has. It is also a beautiful island particularly in the South with its mountains and caves and peninsulas and bays and it gives the impression of having been as it is for a long time.

These are three towns and an island in very different parts

of Australia, each with a strong personal identity of its own. They are all parts of the same country, each one is very different and yet typical of itself.

It was on a Sunday evening less than forty-eight hours after I had arrived in Australia that I caught the sleeper from Perth to Kalgoorlie. Railway stations the world over have the same bustling atmosphere and no matter how much new paint, they still seem rather dusty and dirty. Whistles go, people rush around shouting over their shoulders and train doors slam angrily.

Perth station was no exception. After a twenty minute wait the train shunted into the station and I soon found my berth in a first-class sleeper. There were two bunks, one above the other, a series of light switches, a minute basin under the window with taps that rumbled and produced the merest trickle of water and absolutely nowhere to put a suitcase. I was told I had it to myself and so I appropriated the bottom bunk, but when the train had started a guard came along with a middle-aged Australian who was to have the bunk above me. He was a miner from Kalgoorlie, a man of fairly few words with not much time for other people's words.

For half an hour the train went slowly, but even so as I made my way down to the restaurant car the carriages were swaying a good deal. In Australia each state has retained its own gauge and only very recently has a standard gauge been introduced. In Western Australia the gauge measures three feet six inches and so the swaying was pronounced and on an elderly train the rattling was extreme.

At the end of each carriage where it joined to the next there was a small open-air platform with wrought iron railings where one could stand and look at the countryside. These platforms helped produce a "Western" atmosphere which was to grow much stronger during the next two days. When I eventually arrived in the buffet car at the other end of the train I asked the two girls, both of whom were English, for a drink. I was told that it was Sunday and therefore there was no alcohol. These girls did the cooking and serving from behind a bar in the middle of the carriage. I was hungry by then and the braised steak stew which came out of a tin and was poured over some toast when hot, tasted good even down to the hard peas which had found their way into the tin.

After a considerable time winding its way through the suburbs of Perth, the train picked up speed and we passed first through a belt of cultivated land, but this soon gave way to arid scrubland. The topsoil was a reddish-brown and parched and the scrub consisted of rough bushes and small scrappy gum trees. It was country that irrigation would have been unable to do anything for and its only advantage is in what may lie under the surface in the way of mineral deposits. We had just come into this type of country when night fell, but we awoke to it again the next morning.

For most of the journey there was a constant reminder of the arid lifelessness of the area by a large black pipe, some six feet or more in diameter running beside the railway line. This pipe supplies Kalgoorlie, 500 miles and uphill from Perth, with its entire water supply and starts in the Darling Ranges. Turn off the tap and Kalgoorlie is finished. On the way the train passed through a village which had been destroyed by one of the recent earthquakes. The pipeline had been broken, but for some inexplicable reason the six foot length of pipe which had been crushed did not have to be replaced as the two ends joined together.

Kalgoorlie the next morning was a different world from that of the comfortable suburbs and twentieth century progress which I had left behind in Perth. The solid squat station seemed to combine the atmosphere of uncertainty, the constant companion of the early prospectors, and the exciting prosperity which was the happy lot of some. But there was a touch of rust about both worlds.

In June 1893 an Irishman called Paddy Hannan who was born in County Clare fifty years before discovered the first piece of gold in the area which was to become Kalgoorlie. There is a tree surrounded by white iron fencing which marks the spot where Hannan found this nugget of gold. Hannan remains an ever-present name in Kalgoorlie. There is Hannan's beer, Hannan's Hotel, Hannan's Club and Hannan's Street. In these seventy-five years Kalgoorlie—the name is derived from the native word, *COLGOOLA*—has gone

through the extremes of excitement, prosperity, rising costs
and shrinking yields, and now the new excitement of the
nickel.

It is a dusty, rather dirty town which in places looks to be
almost on the edge of disintegration and there are no signs of
the vast fortunes which its gold has produced. The hotels
were built soon after Kalgoorlie came into being and are
heavily colonial and Victorian and they have hardly been
given a face lift since. The Palace Hotel has an enormous
dining room and a wide leisurely staircase with a public bar
off one side of the hall and the buzz of conversation it
produces echoes disapprovingly round the building. The
shops which have awnings built out over the pavement supply
necessities rather than luxuries. In Hannan's Street alone
there used in the boom years to be thirty-five pubs, none of
which would be short of business, but now there are many
fewer and those that there are show obvious signs of age.

Kalgoorlie is a strictly utilitarian city without any frills.
The fortunes the area has produced have either been taken,
drunk or gambled away, but no one has remained to spend
his money peacefully in Kalgoorlie building and providing the
means to do so. The miners enjoy mostly simple pleasures
and their two main forms of relaxation are gambling and
drinking, and then of course there are the brothels which are
in almost constant use.

The betting shop, the T.A.B., does a good deal of business
and a man I spoke to one evening who used to work in the
T.A.B. told me that much of the gold which is stolen from
the mines finds its way there. The miners come in after their
shifts carrying bundles of clothes and he told me that he was
often asked to put the bundles on the shelves while they
stayed. Occasionally, he would put out his hands expecting
to feel a pile of clothes and sometimes the ore they were
covering was so heavy that he almost dropped everything. He
did not say, but the ore was then presumably used to pay
betting debts or channelled from there to someone who
would pay a price for it. But at the moment more than five
tons of ore have to be brought to the surface for one fine
ounce of gold and so unless a freak stream is found with a
high percentage of gold, gold stealing is a heavy business.

The main gambling in Kalgoorlie is carried on about five

miles out of the town in the scrubland where a small corrugated iron circular shed is the home of "Two-Up". This is a game which was played in many parts of Australia, but it is now illegal although in Kalgoorlie it is carefully run and the police are prepared to tolerate it as long as it causes no trouble. The game could hardly be more simple. Two pennies are placed on a flat piece of wood and gamblers sit or kneel in a circle round a man who throws the pennies high in the air. They bet on whether they both land heads or tails, one of each is no bet. Those playing bet amongst themselves. When I went out in the middle of the afternoon there were about fifty miners in the circle and when the bets were being arranged several people would be walking round the edge of the ring shouting, "fifty dollars heads" or maybe, "twenty dollars tails". If someone wants to accept the bet the man who has offered it hands over his money to his acceptor and when the throw has been made they settle up. Big sums of money are won and lost.

Although this game of "Two-Up" is tolerated by the police the people who run it are careful about who comes and no one is allowed to take photographs of the game. The miners there on a weekday afternoon had come before or after their shifts or on a day off. They were hard weatherbeaten faces with old dusty clothes often covered with the dust of the countryside. They were all faces which seemed to crack when their expression changed. They did not notice the flies as they sat clutching their wad of notes and every so often a man would get up and go either with his hand full of notes or completely empty, but there was seldom an expression of annoyance or satisfaction on his face. The man running the game, the players pay a levy, had a strangely sallow complexion and he was wearing an open shirt and a pair of khaki shorts, but he ran it professionally and smoothly. This corrugated casino had a unique atmosphere with all the tension of gambling, but in the circumstances it was almost a form of elemental combat. It was the only time in Australia, watching the "Two-Up", that I felt out of place. I felt an intruder and half-expected someone to tell me that I was, but it was a fascinating experience.

The Golden Mile, a strip of country about two miles long and half a mile wide, is known as the richest square mile of rock the world over and it has produced a fantastic stream of wealth. The Mile was originally worked by no less than thirty different companies, but now partly as a result of rising costs, shrinking yields and labour shortages and partly because of the tendency of smaller firms to join larger ones, the Mile is operated by four large companies.

From the surface the Golden Mile looks like some deserted battlefield. It is scrubland with the same reddish soil with hundreds of ageing piles of rock and earth rising all over it like a nettlerash. The skyline is broken up with smoke stacks and the head frames of the mines which rise into the air like cone shaped skeletons, as the sky gleams through the lattice work. The area is carved up by a network of roads which link up the small conglomerations of low lying buildings which surround the mine shafts and the tiny corrugated iron buildings which stand alone and apparently lifeless at intervals beside the roads.

At the shaft head the lift cages keep on clattering noisily to the surface where they shed their load of ore or of miners and descend once again to the myriad of tunnels which run beneath the surface at many different levels like some gigantic maze. I went down a mine which is worked by North Kalgurli Ltd. I was given a yellow steel hat with a torch attached to the front of it and after waiting a while the lift rumbled to the surface. I packed into one of the cages with about twenty others including a shift foreman who was my guide. We went down twenty stages to a level of 2,000 feet, stopping once on the way to let another party out. I had been told to switch on my torch and by the time I stepped out into a wide hall of dull grey rock with passages going off in all directions, the temperature had fallen and there was a stillness almost deadness in the atmosphere. Against the rock, voices sounded muffled as the foreman exchanged some words with a group of miners waiting to take the lift back up to the top. Then we set off down one of these passages and my torch was essential. I had to be careful where I walked as there was a twin rail on the ground by which the mined ore was brought back from the face to the lift shaft. We walked for some time passing a number of cross passages and after ten minutes I had lost all sense of direction.

Occasionally we stopped and the foreman whose face was

unforgettably creased, experienced and at the same time distinguished, pointed to a passage entrance whose face was being worked at the time. Sometimes he stopped and picked up a piece of rock and held to the light to show the flickering specks which after the process of crushing would eventually result in gold. By now the tunnel was narrower and the atmosphere rather more dank. We passed two men coming away from the face we were making for. There was a hurried and for me almost unintelligible conversation before they hurried on. Then round a gradual corner the passage led up to a chipped face of grey rock and stopped. There were some small holes in the face and out of them stuck yellow fuse-wire. That evening this face was to be blasted and all the preparations had been made. The foreman spent a minute or two carefully inspecting what had been done. Then he explained the process of blasting and its problems of which the main one is subsidence.

On the way back to the lift shaft I asked him how the miners were able to cope with the constant fog of grey dust which was thick even before the face had been blasted. He slowed fractionally and his face creased into an under-standing grin. "Miner's disease," he said, "it gets us all in the end, it coats the lungs." He was still smiling when he had finished and this was the constant fact of life, or death, with which the miners lived. There was no escaping this one while accidents only happen to a few and are an incidental hazard. The foreman had been a miner all his life, he had known no other existence and indeed there was none other open to him and psillicosis, the miners' disease, was as inevitable as his job.

He was wearing a stained open-necked khaki shirt with the shoulder straps of his dungarees pressing tightly down on his shoulders. He was pleased to show us round but behind it all I suspect that there was a fairly healthy cynicism for another group of visitors from the outside world even though some of them played cricket for the West Indies. Kalgoorlie was the most isolated town and community which I have ever visited and that pipeline alongside the railway helped make it so. But all the same it was far away and alone and therefore has to be self-sufficient. Knowledge of Kalgoorlie was all that the inhabitants could hope to have and they had worked out their own lives to suit themselves. At the moment there is a spirit of excitement caused by the nickel finds around Kalgoorlie, particularly at Kambalda some thirty-five miles South-East of Kalgoorlie. These discoveries have had a marked effect on the inevitable atmosphere of Kalgoorlie where for a long time life has just continued. Roads are being improved, new hotels are being built and once again they are full and generally there is a spirit of expectation in the town. Although the big nickel "finds" are outside Kalgoorlie, it will become the centre for the nickel mining which will bring with it money, people and many of the modern adjuncts of life which follow success.

Although Kalgoorlie is a relatively young town it has a deeply traditional feeling and a walk down Hay Street past the brothels — drums as they are called — is curiously incongruous. There are a dozen or more of the drums and in the evening the girls all dressed and painted to kill sit in the porches. From twenty paces away in the road the majority of them were very attractive and judging from the almost unceasing flow of cars which pulled up in the road outside the miners thought so too. The drums in which the girls live usually house two or three girls and an older woman who runs the drum. The girls themselves come mostly from Sydney although they may have found a Scandinavian name and a broken English accent on the way.

There is about as much nickel in these brothels as there is in the whole of Kambalda for in three years these girls make enough money on which to retire. Even the most monotonous existence becomes attractive when the briefest visit swells funds by twenty dollars. But the drums have to conform to certain rules. They have to close at midnight and the girls have weekly medical inspections. They provide a simple, but effective pleasure and probably contribute to the almost total lack of crime in Kalgoorlie.

The wide streets with a line of trees or lamp posts going down the middle help give Kalgoorlie a Wild West flavour, but for me the lattice-work bar doors which swing wildly whenever a man goes through, brought the town irrevocably onto the cinema screen. It seemed that John Wayne was always about to be the next man through. It was in

Kalgoorlie that I was first introduced to Australian beer, which is similar to lager. It is always served ice-cold in differing sized glasses, all of which are smaller than the English pint mugs. These glasses are called different names through Australia, but in Kalgoorlie the small three ounce glass is a "pony", the five ounce a "glass", the seven ounce a "middy" and the eleven ounce a "pot". After English beer it is difficult to get used to because it is so cold and if one is not used to it, it hurts the back of the throat to drink it fast. But the Australians throw it back and in Hannan's Hotel on my first night in Kalgoorlie playing darts with some of the locals a good deal of beer was being drunk. I was drinking "glasses" to their "middys", but even so I fell behind and when I had a half empty glass and two full ones on the counter and I swallowed another mouthful a hard Australian voice rang out from just behind me. "Go on," it said, "drink the bloody stuff, don't sip it." I tried and nearly choked. Hannan's Hotel was run by one of the great characters of Kalgoorlie, a cheerful man in his early forties who answered to the nickname of Sos. Its origin I never discovered and his shape did not provide the answer. Sos knew everything about Kalgoorlie from the drum with the most beautiful inmates who gave the best value for money, to stories of gold stealing and inside information about the nickel "finds". The only time I ever saw him under pressure was when an Aborigine came into the bar. They are now allowed to be served and this one spent a little time getting out. There were a few Aborigines watching the cricket in Kalgoorlie, but they are a wandering people who play no part in the community life.

Kalgoorlie is a man's community and it is seldom that one sees a woman in a bar and at a party one evening I came across for the first time the way in which the sexes do not intermingle. The men stood talking at one end of the room while the women stood around at the other. The men made no attempt to bring the women into their conversations or indeed to talk to them at all and for their part the women accepted this as normal behaviour. Whether it was in the bar at Hannan's Hotel or with the top echelon of society in the Golf Club, the men of Kalgoorlie were all hard and immensely tough, but human at the same time. They spoke with a rather harsher more pronounced accent than I found anywhere else in the country, but they were always ready to smile. In October Kalgoorlie was very hot, but each afternoon the trees would start to move, blown by the Esperance doctor, a wind which comes up from Esperance in the South of the state, and it would grow refreshingly cooler.

Kalgoorlie had such a unique atmosphere that when I climbed back into the sleeper after two days I felt I was leaving a world I wondered if I would ever see again. Somehow it was like looking at an old Charlie Chaplin film being run at the right speed.

A Greyhound coach called a "Scenicruiser" made a more comfortable but less original journey from Brisbane to Murgon. The air conditioning was important for it was hot and humid and the road surface was smooth.

For the first fifty miles the country was open grassland which went as far as the eye could see on either side of the road, broken only by tall, thin and rather scraggy trees, some growing and some which had died and blown down rather like matches emptied over a huge green carpet. The trees stood in groups of twos and threes but seldom more and never thickly enough to become woodland. The grassland provided pasture for cattle which for once was bright green after the recent storms. Every few miles this pattern was interrupted by small villages which were pleasingly new, but they may have been hiding less sophisticated remnants of the past. Each little village also had its share of bright shining advertisements and again Coca-Cola was linking remote outposts of the world although these particular outposts are now no more than irritating stretches of speed limit on the open road between towns.

Murgon was bigger than any of the villages and the wide main street with the wooden awnings coming out from the shops to the edge of the pavements and the colourful signs offering watchmakers and hairdressers and jewellers, in addition to the large number of parked cars gave it a certain standing. At the end of the Main Street stood a colourful sign saying, "Welcome to Murgon the Hub of the South Burnett". It had a map showing the whereabouts of the town and in small letters at the top was written, "Another Murgon Chamber of Commerce Project". Down the side was a list of things the town had to offer, including Scenic Tours and Range Shooting; the things it has, including sewerage, abattoirs and an Olympic Swimming Pool; the things it produces, including peanuts, linseed and tropical fruit; and then some data which put the population at 5,000. In the same street there was a war memorial which was a strong reminder that however remote Murgon may have seemed it was not as far away as all that. The hotel had recently had a motel wing built on to it and it was as comfortable as any motel I stayed in. A few decades were thrown away however on the short walk to the old part of the hotel and the bar. The names of the beer, like the names of the glasses were constantly changing in Australia and here it was Castlemaine beer and I drank it out of a schooner.

The excitement caused by the visit of the West Indians was of course high. The locals were going to see in action players who had until then been only names. Soon after we arrived I went for a walk through the little town. I was in a short road with neat little houses built on stilts on either side when I heard an angry female shout. By the steps leading up to the door of the house on my right an ample Australian woman of about forty who was watering a piece of garden shouted to someone, "Go and have a look at the fire." Immediately a twelve year old girl came running from behind the house up to the front gate, where she picked up her bicycle and shouted back over her shoulder, "I have looked at the fire. I'm going to have a look at the West Indians." The girl was bicycling hard when her mother shouted after her shaking her fist at the same time, "I'll give you the West Indians," and disappeared angrily behind the house. But cricket won the day and the little girl continued to pedal hard for the hotel.

The one-day match drew a good crowd. The small wooden stand was packed and people were sitting all round the ground behind the boundary. To the right of the stand were the wooden railed holding yards for the rodeo horses with spectators sitting on the railings. On the far side of the ground there were a number of Aborigines and throughout the day farmers kept on turning up on their horses to watch for a few minutes before riding off again. There were a number of trees around the ground, all of which looked as if they were finding existence a struggle. Their names were rather better than their appearances; there were Blue Gums, Spotted Gums, Iron Barks and Silky Oaks, but they helped give the ground some atmosphere. In the distance the country went down a gradual valley and up again. In the middle distance there was a small field of dark green lucerne which looked vividly unreal in the parched surroundings. Through the day the life of the farmers went on in spite of the cricket. During the afternoon a farmer using his car drove some of his cattle into the lucerne for them to feed. Then twenty minutes later before they could become bloated they were driven out again. There was another lot of cattle on the arid grassland and they were twice moved to a different area and on the other side of the valley a tractor looking like an ant crawled backwards and forwards for most of the day.

The Aborigines come from a nearby Aborigine Settlement called Cherbourg. I met two of the Australian schoolteachers from the Settlement during the afternoon and the name apparently comes from the Aboriginal word Cheaubourg meaning Water-hole. The story has it that when the name was first sent to be printed it came back as Cherbourg and maybe the printer was more familiar with the French port.

Murgon has the strong yet sympathetic atmosphere that I think one often finds in agricultural communities. On the only evening I spent in Murgon there was a big dance at the Town Hall in honour of the West Indians. First there was a buffet supper, when a large number of civic dignitaries made interminable speeches of welcome, but this part of the proceedings was for men only. When it was over the doors swung open and the girls and the band appeared. But it was a long time before any attempt was made by the men to break up the women. The dancing therefore made a stuttering start, but eventually it got properly under way and it went on well into the next day, taking a delightfully old-fashioned form. There was no modern beat music, but a succession of Foxtrots and Waltzes and Barn Dances and Prides of Arran, all of which were beautifully danced by girls in outstanding dresses even if the hemlines were a little lower than in the cities. It was a tremendously gay evening and for Murgon it was in honour of a unique occasion, and for the West Indians too for they may never again be asked to try and cope with the Pride of Arran. When they finished serving alcohol at the party everyone walked over the road to the pub which stayed open as long as was wanted. It was a night when the closing laws could be justifiably waived.

Murgon was a simple but delightfully friendly place. It had no pretensions or illusions about itself. It provided its people with a good but simple way of life. For city dwellers the pleasures might, in spite of that notice, have seemed sparse, but Murgon enjoys its pleasures to the full, only it does not allow them to get in the way of the main purposes of life which are cattle, potatoes, peanuts and linseed. When we left Murgon we were driven to a grass landing strip where a chartered two engine aeroplane picked us up. A lot of people from Murgon came to see us off and they waved until the aeroplane was almost out of sight.

As the aeroplane begins its descent into Mildura the land beneath is rocky and lifeless, but at the height when cars on the road suddenly look like cars, this gives way to the vineyards. On both sides of the aeroplane the carefully husbanded rich green vines stretched in all directions in a maze of parallel lines and right angles. From the air it was an oasis. The Airport was small, but with a regular service of smaller aeroplanes bringing grey suited business men up to the vineyards.

The Mildura Wineries have turned Mildura into a household word in Australia. In the last few years the Australians have acquired a taste for wines and accordingly the wine industry has grown enormously. Irrigation came to Mildura towards the end of the last century when two Canadian brothers, George and W.B. Chaffey saw the possibilities the Murray River gave to the area and the Victorian Government of the time leased them the land and it was they who first introduced grapes to the area. The Chaffeys, magnificent house now turned into a hotel stands handsomely in the middle of the town. In the meantime, the wine industry has grown into big business.

Mildura has acquired some of the sophisticated gloss of a rapidly expanding commercial community. The production of wine itself is a process which cannot be hurried. During the grape harvest the work is carried on at fever pitch until it is finished, but then comes the complicated business of blending and the long wait for maturity. On the other hand, more land has come under irrigation and a much bigger area is now growing grapes. Accordingly every aspect of the process has grown and more skilled workers have been needed and there has been a continual pattern of growth in Mildura.

There is not the same feeling of isolation in Mildura as in the other up country towns I visited, and outside influences are affecting the pattern of life in the town. In the two days I was there I ran into a number of business men up from Adelaide and Melbourne and as many local people who had only just returned from one of the big cities. I also met some young people whose homes were in Mildura, but who worked elsewhere and had returned for a holiday. The wine industry brought the Airport which in its turn opened up all kinds of possibilities.

The wide streets and comfortable old houses were evidence of the prosperity of the period which began with the Chaffeys. The older houses were beautifully maintained and gave the town a certain standing as well as creating an impression of permanence. The "new" is there as well: The Travelodge chain of Motels have built in Mildura and more mundanely there are large housing estates and the small modern stores which service them.

I was not so conscious of the toughness in the Australian character which was noticeable in the other small towns. The success of the town had worn away a lot of rough edges while the Winery had had to import many of its skilled workers. In conversation and ideas most people were looking outside Mildura, and the town had no feeling of insularity.

The Working Men's Club is the focal point for much of the social life in the town. It is a large and extremely well appointed building and one evening there was the usual party there. Downstairs is the famous winding bar nearly 400 feet long and still growing with more than fifty taps. The challenge to drink a glass from each in the same evening is often accepted, but less often completed. That night the band played beat music as well as square dances and when

Seymour Nurse took over the microphone and gave a fine take-off of Louis Armstrong, the whole room soon joined in and 'Hello Dolly' rang out of the windows. The words and the tune were known and it was natural to join in.

The second morning there I was driven out at nine o'clock to be shown round the Wineries. They are to be found just out of the town high up on the Victorian bank of the Murray River. The white buildings were beautifully tidy and clean and at first sight it did not look like anything more than a crop of new farm buildings. There were gum trees growing everywhere and it was only when I got inside the buildings that I knew what was happening. Five minutes inside the one where the brandy is maturing left me in no doubt for after a few deep breaths I began to feel half drunk, the fumes were so strong. The methods were carefully explained by one of the directors who had himself spent a certain time in the vineyards of France learning the trade and the methods were, I am sure, every bit as efficient. The end product is very acceptable too and more reasonably priced, but although the same grapes are used the Australians will probably never produce wines to compare with the best which come out of the continent of Europe. But drinking cold Moselle—the Australian wines all have the European names—at ten o'clock in the morning in the boardroom of the Midlura Wineries was a delightful and invigorating experience.

When I left Mildura I felt it was important to Australia and that it was enthusiastically aware of this. Kalgoorlie is, of course, more important but Kalgoorlie wore its importance with an inevitable shrug of the shoulders.

Tasmania is a state of Australia, but it is also an island with its own individual characteristics both geographically and mentally. It is very different from the mainland. It is one of the most mountainous countries in the world, some of the scenery is exceptional, it has a strong sense of history and in many ways a marked similarity to England. The people as a whole are quieter and more reflective than on the mainland and life does not have the same sharp competitive edge.

There can be few cities in the world set in such beautiful surroundings as Hobart. The wide estuary of the Derwent River provides one of the finest natural harbours in the world and produces a perfect foreground for the city. At the back, Mount Wellington stands solid and impressive, 4,165 feet high and from the top it offers the most spectacular view in Tasmania looking down over Hobart and following the Derwent out to the sea. The city is a mottled patchwork of coloured roofs, but it is full of trees and there is a lot of open parkland. The physical pattern of the city is the same as that in the mainland cities with the older buildings forming rectangles of banks and so on in the centre and being called after Macquarie, Collins, Bathurst and many others. Then the bungaloid suburbs go back from the river to the Mount Wellington on one side of the water and sprawl over the low hills on the other. It is a city with an atmosphere which faithfully reflects the tempo and spirit of the South of the island.

The South of Tasmania around Hobart is visually the most exciting part of the island. There are endless drives from Hobart through rugged coastal scenery with all the various wonders of nature. The seventy odd miles from Hobart to Port Arthur the old convict settlement on the Tasman Peninsula contains almost everything. The road passes over narrow causeways with the sea lapping only five yards away on each side of the road, the beaches are perfect and no better setting for a picnic of cold lobster and iced white wine was ever invented. On the right of the car the coastline unwinds in a succession of bays and inlets and peninsulas and there are many small islands just off the coast. Somehow each view is better than the last. Eaglehawk Neck, a narrow strip, takes one onto the Tasman Peninsula which, but for this strip, would be an island and it helped make Port Arthur such an effective convict settlement. Just by the Neck there are four freaks of nature: Tasman's Arch a bridge made by nature out of solid stone, The Devil's Kitchen which is the pool of water which takes the backlash from the Blowhole on stormy days, the Blowhole itself, a small hole in the rock through which the tide comes, with a tremendous roar when a gale is blowing, and the Tesselated Pavement, a stretch of rock so engraved that it looks like a giant pavement.

The country now gets rougher and the road narrower before winding downhill into Port Arthur. There the ruined convict settlement stands peacefully in the sun. The church which has been gutted by bush fires stands roofless on an island in the road. By the side of the bay the shell of the penitentiary remains, gutted inside by fire, but with the bars in front of the windows still making it horrifyingly austere. Across the water there is the Isle of the Dead where many of the convicts ended up. The old hospital, the Guard House, the Governor's House and by a strange quirk of fate, the Lunatic Asylum now used as the Tasman Council Chambers, still survive. Port Arthur is an awe-inspiring sight. From what remains it is not difficult to imagine the desperate scenes of human misery which were enacted in its precincts. There still stands in the middle of Port Arthur an elderly signpost which might have come out of Treasure Island. Its four arms read, Half Moon Bay, Remarkable Cove 4, Point Puer 3, Safety Cove 3.

The road going South-West from Hobart down the Huon Valley is not so spectacular, but it is still beautiful. Now the road is on the other side of the Derwent and the water gleams from the left while on each side of the road there is nothing but orchards. The first apple was planted in Tasmania by Lieutenant William Bligh in 1788 and from such small beginnings has grown one of the principle industries of the island. The road crosses the Huon River and passes through many modern villages each the local centre for the fruit growing industry. Eventually the road turns right and winds through a dense jungle of tall, tightly packed trees and the atmosphere becomes very eerie. After a mile or two like this the road stops and there is a narrow path leading into the trees which is the entrance of the Hastings Caves. Walking into these caves is like entering another world as the grotesque shapes and fantastic formations appear skilfully lit up to produce the best effect. On the rocky platform above the entrance to the cave and the woods where it is possible to catch sight of the elusive lyre birds, it seemed to be ten degrees colder than when I got out of my car.

Going North from Hobart the road leads through more fruit growing country with the Derwent still on one side. The road goes through New Norfolk which proudly displays the Bush Hotel which holds the oldest licence in Australia, up past the salmon ponds at Plenty where may be surprisingly, trout are bred in vast numbers. The first Brown and Rainbow Trout in the Southern Hemisphere was successfully raised at these ponds in 1864. This led to the stocking of lakes and streames in Australia and New Zealand. Around the ponds are trees—poplars, oaks and elms which could have been lifted straight out of the English countryside. Hops are grown in this area too and the conical oast houses give it more than just a passing similarity to parts of Kent.

Eventually the road comes to the National Park which is a home for Tasmania's fascinating and varied animal life. The Russell Falls are in the National Park and so is Mount Mawson which between July and October produces the best snow in the island for the skiers.

The Midland Highway is the quickest and easiest way of covering the 124 miles from Hobart to Launceston, but the Lake Highway where for much of the way the road is just sand and stone is much the more picturesque route. It winds endlessly through the wild countryside which is a mixture of grass and woodland with the occasional enormous flock of sheep with the shepherds and their dogs the only sign of life. It is a rugged and beautiful country with the hills all the time changing the blackcloth and presenting new panoramas. Then the lakes appear, great steely grey masses of water coldly reflecting the neighbouring countryside and producing some exceptional views which it seemed a tragedy to leave. The different foliage of the trees and the many gay wild flowers by the side of the road all contributed to the effect.

Then twenty miles or so short of Launceston the road joined a more modern highway and although the countryside was still surprisingly English, even down to the hawthorn hedgerows, the roar of the lorries showed that this end of the island housed Tasmania's main industries. Launceston is a friendly city without the physical beauty of Hobart and with a rather harder more commercial approach to life. The pace is quicker and although the Tamar River offers many attractive views there are not the exciting extremes of the South of the island. But after the constant whirl of aeroplane journeys and Test Matches and feverishly cabled stories, Tasmania was the idyllic place to get away from it all.

Instinct and discipline

It was in this environment so different from their own and yet in many ways as distinctive that the West Indians travelled and played cricket for nearly four and a half months. When the West Indians came down from their aeroplane in Perth in the middle of October there were a few new and unknown faces, but the nucleus of the side had ridden through the streets of Melbourne cheered on their way by half a million people when Worrell's side left Australia in 1961. The anticipation of Sobers' party was strong. No one expected that they would recapture the drama and excitement of the previous tour for these things seldom happen twice, let alone twice running, but the West Indians are instinctive, volatile cricketers to whom nothing is impossible.

The tour followed a course of exaggerated extremes. From the way they started in Perth the stories that this side was past its best seemed to be so many ill-founded rumours. Hall and Griffith bowled out the first 7 Western Australians for 39, Sobers played what may well have been the best innings of even his career; they beat Western Australia and then only lost to the combined eleven after a declaration in a match which produced any amount of high class and thrilling cricket. Once again the West Indians had fired the imagination of the Australian public.

By the time they arrived in Adelaide to shake Sir Donald Bradman's hand at the airport, many of the West Indians had let this early success go to their heads. For them it was now just a question of waiting until the Test Matches began. The preliminaries were finished, they thought. For the next three days they played cricket as if engaged only in a gentle form of exercise in the open air. They could not be bothered to apply themselves and concentrate and they were beaten by ten wickets in three days. As a result they heard some harsh words from the captain and the manager and spent the next two games starting all over again. When they arrived in Brisbane ten days before the First Test they were at least back on an even keel although the rumours surrounding the departure of Sobers to Melbourne for a week had a disquieting effect. He was however back in time for the Test Match which the West Indies won comfortably, largely as a result of winning the toss on a wicket which broke up as the game went on and Sobers and Gibbs used it well to spin Australia to defeat.

It was the high moment of the tour for the West Indians. There followed up-country matches in Mackay and Mildura and inevitably the players relaxed away from the tensions of Test cricket. Then they came back to Adelaide just before Christmas for the return South Australia game and far from knuckling down again to the hard business which is Test cricket, they fielded a very weak bowling side, never got down to it, and were almost beaten.

It was therefore not at all that surprising that after Lawry had won the toss on a slightly green wicket at Melbourne on Boxing Day and put the West Indies in, that the same symptoms appeared and that they were all out early on the second day for 202. The experienced players could not produce the effort to fight for runs, they got out to some outrageous strokes and there was a general lack of determination. The feebleness of some of the older players on this day was illustrated by Fredericks who, playing in his first Test Match, with his limited technique, batted all through the first day for 70 not out. If he could fight through the day batting as he did, the others could certainly have done so too.

The West Indies side which took the field on the third day was understandably apprehensive. Their fears were then systematically underlined by Lawry and Chappell and Australia built up a lead of 211 and the West Indies, showing all the same symptons when they batted again, were beaten by an innings with a day to spare. The Australians bowled steadily against batsmen who were fast acquiring a neurosis. The Third Test at Sydney was minutely repetitious of the Second except that the West Indies won the toss and batted first on a glorious wicket and that this time Lawry and Walters were the main run-scorers for Australia. The match crept 20 minutes into the fifth day, Australia winning by ten wickets. For three and a half days the Fourth Test at Adelaide followed an identical pattern, with Australia building up a first innings lead of 257. Then for the first time since Brisbane, the West Indies batsmen began to fight. They turned their deficit into a lead of 359 and left Australia 344 minutes to get them. They failed by twenty runs and the West Indies by one wicket to bowl them out. It was the brief and final return to the type of cricket Australia had been hoping for from these West Indians. Finally in Sydney the young, efficient and in parts brilliant Australians ruthlessly exposed the many shortcomings of the West Indians in spite of a faint but clear echo of the past given right at the end by an exciting hundred from Nurse.

It may not be quite true to say that the Australians have an obsession for victory, but they do not like coming second. Defeat is minutely analysed and the lessons from it are learned while victory is accepted as a side or a person's right and proper reward. This does not fit cricket alone, for the Australians I met, no matter what sport they were interested or involved in, victory was the end object on the basis that if a game is worth playing it is worth winning. Theirs is a fundamentally different approach to the West Indies' and also different from the English approach where a lot of games take place outside of league tables and the other adjuncts of competition.

Australian cricket is geared to winning. When the selectors meet which they usually do by interstate link-up telephone conversations, they pick the eleven best cricketers in the country and then choose a captain from among them. It may be as a result of this approach that international cricket is much more within the grasp of and less of a mystery to Australian club cricketers. In England the gap between First-Class cricket and any other form is vast and almost unattainable but in Australia the basis of their cricket is club or grade or district cricket which is played over two days on following Saturdays. A look at a Sunday paper in Sydney or Melbourne reveals lots of famous names in the previous day's local cricket scores.

It is therefore possible for a really good young player to come into his first grade side at the start of the season, score a couple of hundreds and to go on in a matter of weeks to the

State side where equal success leads to Test cricket. This relative nearness of Test cricket or of its possibility means that most of Australian cricket at whatever stage of the overall graduated scale it is played, has considerable relative importance. The atmosphere of the cricket at any step on the ladder is always preparing for the next step and this ladder goes on up in logical stages until the highest point is reached. At no stage is the young player having to stop and start all over again.

The structure of their cricket combined with the natural toughness and determination in the Australian character explains why they are such tremendous competitors when it comes to Test cricket. Australian sides always seem to use their chances, the last three in the order have an irritating habit of batting extraordinarily well, they do not drop catches and it is a surprise if they are beaten.

The young Australian side which came to maturity in this series combined all these reasons and characteristics both individually and generally. It was amazing to see how much they had learned from the tour of England and how they applied these lessons in a methodical and unemotional way. They had all worked at their cricket no matter how much natural talent they had and this way as little as possible is left to chance. Their subsequent failure in South Africa was largely the result of a massive crisis of confidence in the touring party which was not explicable solely in cricketing terms.

During the series each member of the side made significant contributions to their success. They were captained efficiently and clinically by Lawry who found that he now had under him a good enough side for him to take a rather more aggressive line. He put the West Indies in at Melbourne and working so well it gave him the confidence in himself as well as his side to allow himself to become a more flexible tactician. Walking in his angular way from mid-off to mid-off Lawry sums up the determination of the Australian side. With a bat in his hands he scored 667 runs in the series and he more than anyone else saw to it after the First Test at Brisbane that the West Indies never had a second chance.

When the West Indies think back to this tour or have nightmares about it they will see visions of any combination of Walters, Lawry or Chappell who between them scored over

1,850 runs in the series. In England six months earlier Chappell had looked a good player being about the best of the Australians on the awkward wickets, but now he showed that he was more than just a good cricketer. Cricket runs in Chappell's blood for he is the grandson of Victor Richardson who captained Australia in the 1930's. Watching Chappell walk out through the Pavilion gates or sitting and talking in the bar of the Arkaba Hotel in Adelaide, his home town, one can see the toughness in his character which goes a long way to making him the cricketer he is. He is at the same time a gentle man, but there are no frills to his character and he will go on to make Australia an efficient captain in the uncompromising mould of Australian captains.

While the early part of the tour belonged exclusively to Chappell who in all matches scored more than 1,000 runs against the West Indies, the last half belonged equally exclusively to Walters. After missing the First Test because of a leg injury Walters then played innings of 76, 118, 110, 50, 242 and 103 in his six innings in the last four Tests.

Walters made a remarkable impact on Test cricket when he played against the MCC in 1965/66, but then he had to go into the army for two years. When he came out he found himself almost immediately on a tour of England without too much practice behind him. The difficulties of damp English wickets and the ball moving around off the seam undermined not only his technique, but also his self-confidence. He became bottom handed and rather two-eyed and getting back to Australia he set about on the hard, true wickets putting all this behind him.

When he came into the side at Melbourne he made 76 after Lawry and Chappell had taken all the bite out of the bowling and he did not make them very well. I got the impression watching him then that he was acutely conscious that his own Test career was at stake in that innings and that it was his mental approach as much as anything which let him down. But in spite of this and the way he played he had the determination to stay there and score enough runs to build up this confidence. He looked a completely different player in the Third Test at Sydney and continued to improve to the end of the series when he established a new record by scoring a double and a single century in the same Test.

Long before the end he had corrected the bad habits he had fallen into in England and he had become a supremely efficient batsman. He is not a glamorous strokeplayer like Redpath or Sheahan, but he is a batsman who hits the ball equally well off either foot and on Australian wickets has a compact defence. But it will be interesting to see if he makes runs with this sort of consistency in England. He is a batsman who moves into position fairly early and although it was impossible to fault him during this series, he could come unstuck again when he returns to the problems of English wickets. But Walters is another Australian who sets his sights on success and he is a great fighter.

In the final analysis the West Indies lost this series because they dropped their catches, although this was only another obvious symptom of a side which was playing badly. If they had scored enough runs they probably would not have dropped the catches, but these three Australian batsmen did not give them the chance to rectify the mistakes. In the field the Australians were all impressive in their own ways. In spite of his ambling gait Lawry moves with fair speed in the mid off, mid on region and throughout the series he often threw the stumps down when the batsmen were going for short singles. His catching too was extremely safe.

Chappell has developed into a slip field to rank with Simpson, his predecessor in this position. He is well-balanced and he does not obviously prefer one side to the other and he manages to get two hands to most things. Again Chappell is not a showman in the field, but very little gets past him. Walters misses little too whether fielding close or in the cover or mid-wicket areas. He is a quick mover and a beautiful thrower. There is nothing that these three Australians leave to doubt except possibly Chappell and Walters' bowling. Chappell bowls leg-breaks and although he turns them appreciably he does not have enough bowling to be consistently accurate. South Australia have a fine leg-spinner in Jenner who played a big part in the West Indians defeat by South Australia. This type of bowling was always a worry to the West Indians for they were unable to read the spin and they none of them dared to use their feet to get to the pitch. Walters hardly bowled his medium fast seamers during the series and his bowling had gone off enough for the selectors to say that they could not consider him as a third seamer in the side.

While these three batsmen were the main spectres for the West Indians, their batsmen will not enjoy dreaming about McKenzie, Connolly or Gleeson. The West Indies never scored the runs of which they were capable and Gleeson probably more than any other of the Australian bowlers was responsible for this. He presented them with a new problem spinning the ball with his middle finger tucked back against the palm of his right hand. Sobers was the only West Indian who appeared to be able to read Gleeson with any certainty and it took him some time. Always keeping to a tidy length off his short run and with an economical action Gleeson built up a psychological hold over the batsmen.

Batsman after batsman peered myopically down the wicket at him thrusting bat and front pad hopefully forward without getting near enough to the pitch to smother what spin there was. On these wickets Gleeson was never able to get much turn and it was only because of the West Indians own shortsightedness that he had the effect he did. When he first played against them in the New South Wales match in November, Camacho and Butcher started off against him as if they were staying in a haunted house and while expecting that every bump was a ghost they were determined to be brave. For nearly an hour they threw their bats at him, but without ever moving their feet. The ball often went in the air, but it fell clear of the fielders. Then after an interval Camacho holed out at deep mid-wicket and the batsmen now began to grope and Gleeson was allowed to bowl himself into the Test side.

The problem of Gleeson was one which these same West Indian batsmen must have solved a few years earlier. One felt that all they needed to do in the pavilion was coolly to work the problem out and maybe if the majority of their batsmen had been younger and still playing for a place in the side they would have done. As it was Gleeson went on playing the part of the ghost with great success until the second innings of the Fourth Test at Adelaide when Carew realised that he was not turning the ball and hit him straight and very hard, but by then it was too late. A little collective thought inspired perhaps by the captain might and should have removed this obstacle a great deal earlier; at any rate they should have tried to solve this problem.

The West Indies' original collapse at Melbourne was inspired by McKenzie who returned to his best form during the series and took thirty wickets. He is a big, strong man with a wide chest and a superb action which is a perfect study for all boys. He has a short run, but all his increasing momentum is channelled perfectly into his wide delivery stride, the power coming from a combination of his body which from the waist upwards is bent back at the start of this final stride, and his shoulders. In the field McKenzie is an almost lethargic mover, but with a powerful throw and a safe pair of hands. He walks in big strides with a thick head of fair hair which from time to time he pushes back into place. He also has the usual fast bowlers' worry with his shirt sleeve. He does not swing the ball much, but with such a lively action McKenzie always seems to be able to get that extra inch of bounce out of even the deadest wicket and this is what gives him that little bit extra. For such an aggressive bowler though, McKenzie is a strangely quiet, gentle character.

Connolly on the other hand is no quicker than fast medium, but with superb control and being so different from McKenzie he benefits from him, partly because the batsman may subconsciously relax. But Connolly's use to Lawry is twofold for he is not only a dangerous new ball bowler, but he can also be used as a stock bowler to contain and he is amazingly difficult to score against. He has a relaxed run up and then seems to spring to life about a yard from the wicket. As he delivers the ball his front hand shakes at the batsman and he puts everything into his action.

His best spell of the series came on the first day of the First Test at Brisbane when after tea with the second new ball he took 4 for 12 in 5.6 overs. The West Indies had gone into tea at 187 for one but at the close of play were 267 for 9. It was a remarkable piece of bowling by Connolly who in the humid atmosphere moved the ball in the air and off the seam with superb control. Connolly is also probably the best dressed of all first-class cricketers. Wherever he was, at an airport in the early morning or at a restaurant in the evening he always looks immaculate in a suit cut in the modern style, and he is very much the extrovert to go with it.

These six played the biggest part in Australia's success, but the others in the side also had their moments. Redpath when dropped down the order played a glorious innings of 80 in the Third Test and he made his first Test hundred in the last which was also at Sydney. Stackpole took on Redpath's job as Lawry's partner with obvious relish and played three consecutive innings of 50 or more in his entertainingly aggressive style. Freeman had his moments with both bat and ball, scoring 76 in the Third Test and twice hitting Sobers' stumps in his tally of 13 wickets. The one enigma during the series was Sheahan who showed in brief glimpses that he is the most attractive and elegant strokeplayer the Australians have, but he never found form. So often he reached about 30 and then got himself out in some careless way and gave the impression that he has not as yet got quite the concentration he needs. His fielding in the covers was one of the joys of the series. Lloyd came to Australia with the reputation of being about the finest fieldsman in the world, but in the five Tests Sheahan constantly fielded the better, the most noticeable difference being in the throwing. Lloyd is a marvellous thrower off balance but his normal throw did not have the pinpoin̄   arman's farewell   natches, but never kept well and was replaced for the last by Taber from New South Wales who had a fine first game and is obviously going to be Australia's wicket-keeper for some long time. The only other Australian to play in a Test was Mallett the off-spinner who was in the side at Brisbane. But on a helpful wicket for an off-spinner Lawry handled him strangely giving him a total of four overs in the West Indies second innings in three different spells. This was odd because Gibbs had already shown what there was in the wicket for an off-spinner. He was after that replaced by Freeman who became the third seamer in the side, but Mallett is definitely the better cricketer of the two and soon he must become a regular member of their side.

All these Australians have arrived at the top as a result above all of hard work which has enabled them to develop their talents and at the same time to climb up the graduated scale of Australian cricket. The West Indians also work at their cricket, but because of their temperaments the word seems to take on another meaning. Cricket in the West Indies is a less stylised game and the basis on which most of their

batsmen build their game originally is eye rather than
technique. Technique comes later as the batsman reaches
more sophisticated levels. But this basic dependence on eye
never leaves them. From the village streets in Barbados to a
Test Match in, say, Melbourne is a long way and the lessons
which were learned in the original circumstances and the
methods they led to can never be completely forgotten
because they appeal to the same instinct.

Of course when a West Indian reaches Test Match cricket
many of the rough edges in technique have been smoothed
over and temperamentally they are steadier. The West Indies
side which first under Worrell and then Sobers had such a
fine record during the early 1960's was about as efficient a
side as there can ever have been. They had a man for every
situation, batting or bowling, they were efficient and
technically there were virtually no flaws. But most of them
still played the game by ear rather than design and here lay
their main attraction and also their main weakness. Even
though they were winning consistently they were still an
unpredictable side who had retained the sense of adventure
and fun which they show playing cricket at a far lower level
on the corners or on rough pieces of ground in Barbados or
Berbice or anywhere else in the West Indies.

While this partly explains their success it also to a large
degree accounts for their failures. When everything is going
right the wave of enthusiasm is all-enveloping and gets higher
and higher, but when things are going wrong it subsides at an
even faster rate. In Australia they were the weaker of the two
sides, but in losing the series as badly as they did they were
the victims of their own temperaments which do not allow
them to regroup mentally and take stock of the situations
and problems in front of them when things start going wrong.
In a way they are like impulsive gamblers who begin to lose
and go on doubling and redoubling their stakes regardless. In
each of the last four Tests when things were going from bad
to worse for them, their batsmen including the older and
more experienced, got out playing even more outrageous
shots the worse the situation became. Their temperaments
would not allow them to buckle down and slowly to fight
their way back onto an even keel. It is no more their way of
cricket than it is their way of life.

When things are going well for them this approach is fine,

but when as now it was going badly it made the side appear to be at times almost a laughing stock. There were some specific cricket reasons to explain why they were beaten as they were, but they all really fit under this general heading. The captaincy fell some way short of the standard set by Worrell, the older players were not all willing to fight as once they had done and the party allowed their early success at Brisbane to go straight to their heads and were unable to come back to earth until it was too late.

As a cricketer Sobers is supreme and would have been supreme in any age, but as a captain the sharp instinct on which his whole game is based leaves him. At the wicket Sobers' loose-limbed and lithe strokeplay combined with his superb technical efficiency is impossible to pinpoint in a word. Efficiency and beauty so seldom go together and Sobers' batting is given its beauty by the natural grace of all his movements. In all that he does Sobers is an uncut stone with many facets, but once a man is captain of a side and a losing side at that, instinct has to give way to practicality based on deliberate thoughts which must be directed at solving the problem.

As a player Sobers has never known serious failure as almost every other cricketer alive has experienced. His amazing talents have enabled him to overcome every obstacle he has faced. He has never therefore had to work out the game for himself in the way of all other cricketers and this has meant that he is unaware of many of cricket's problems. When he took over the captaincy from Worrell he found himself in charge of a side which to all intents and purposes captained itself because all the integral members were great players who did what was expected of them. It was a matter of changing the bowling and waiting. But now, although the instinct remained in these same players, age was beginning to take its toll and while they themselves may not have been over-prepared to sit down and work out their own limitations, Sobers himself still at the peak, was unable to understand and to advise.

A captain is much more vulnerable when he has a losing side under him for the minute to minute tactical decisions are so crucially important. He needs to understand his own players more as well as having an acute eye for spotting the weaknesses of opponents. For a lot of the time he is of necessity making the best of a bad job and it is important that he should be aware of the options in front of him. Each of the last four Tests in this series saw Australia score more than 500 runs in their first innings with more than one long partnership. When Lawry and Walters or Chappell were in with the quality of his attack Sobers main hope was to contain and hope that the batsmen would get themselves out, but so often he seemed to have no idea how to do this and no plan which he was trying to put into action. Early on the second day at Melbourne when Lawry and Chappell were batting, Sobers, wandering from mid-off to mid-off appeared to have lost control.

He did not appreciate the needs of the situation and this was very apparent with his batting. He had a fine tour and made a lot of big scores in his own exciting way, but in the Tests he consistently went in at number six. It was soon obvious that he was not going to get the runs he expected from his main batsmen and therefore it became important that Sobers the one player who was going to play up to expectations should give the others a lead. If Sobers is at the wicket for an hour and a half in any cricket match the bowlers are going to be suffering. Sobers should therefore have quickly seen that his place was at number four. If he had batted there he would have gone in with three more established batsmen to follow, all of whom would have profited from his example. He would almost certainly have taken charge of the Australian bowling which would in any case have been less on top having taken two wickets than they were later when they had taken four. As it was when Sobers came in four wickets were usually down for around a hundred and he was committed to a salvage operation with very little batting to come. In the old days with Hunte, Kanhai, Nurse and Butcher making runs consistently he could afford the luxury of a place at six, but no longer. It was ironical that the only time he batted at four, in the first innings of the last Test, he had a leg injury and it was the one occasion when, with a blank day on the morrow, he should have held himself back in the hope that the others could survive that evening so that his leg would be better two days later. He came in at the fall of the second wicket, found he was under a handicap, played some risky strokes before being caught behind cutting at a good length ball.

Sobers' upbringing in the West Indies side coincided with a time when they were usually winning by attacking all the time and this has helped to develop further an already aggressive instinct where cricket is concerned. He has a strong will coupled probably with a streak of obstinacy. Another of his failings as a captain was his remoteness to his side. On free days Sobers was hardly ever seen with his players, he seldom practised with them, spending a great deal of time on the golf course and therefore did not lead by example. His strangest act came just before the First Test when instead of coming up to Brisbane with the party from Sydney he went to Melbourne for a week on a business trip. This was of course big news, a captain deserting his side just before the First Test when there were still a lot of questions of selection still to be answered, and the publicity was hardly encouraging for the other players. They won the First Test however and so no more was heard of this. But is is hard to deny that a touring captain's main responsibility and business is to be with his party especially just before the start of a series when tensions begin to mount.

After winning the First Test Sobers could perhaps by using his own ability as the inspiration at least have enabled the West Indies to draw the series. But Sobers is the man he is and therefore the cricketer he is and no one would want it to be any other way. It does, however, mean that he is the captain he is and it is sad for the West Indies that a player with so much ability and experience which gives him potentially so much to offer for the future of West Indies cricket should be unable to do so. But Sobers comes from the West Indies and there is a lot of the West Indies in him.

The effect of his captaincy, or lack of it, was that his side disintegrated as a team and became eleven individuals. They pursued their own reasons for success and the frustration of continuous failure caused the side to fall apart even faster. But all the well known players showed in their own distinctive ways that they still had the ability to play Test cricket. A strong captain who could have welded them into a unit and made them fight might have channelled this ability into victory. It was interesting to speculate on the progress of this series if Lawry and Sobers had changed camps.

It was a disillusioning tour for many of the West Indians and a difficult one for the younger untried players. Fast bowlers, like prime ministers, tend to go on too long and this was true of Hall and Griffith. The long run and all the familiar gestures were still there, but the pace and rhythm had departed forever. Kanhai, Nurse and Butcher went through the motions of the extravagant strokes which sent spectators into ecstasy a decade before, but often now they were beating thin air and the best and last reward was an outside edge. Hendricks, still tidy, found it harder to get across on the leg side; after Brisbane Gibbs found that against quick-footed batsmen on such splendid batting wickets, there was not much he could do. In the past Hall and Griffith usually managed to soften up the batting for Gibbs, but now he had to do it on his own and in defence he pushed the ball through quicker and quicker. The sharp edge of success which is a combination of youth and fitness and in the case of the West Indies instinct and enthusiasm as well as ability, had been blunted; but careless husbandry was now letting it rust unnecessarily.

It was hard for the young members of the party for they were seeing cricketers whom they and all other West Indians had worshipped for ten years, go the way of all flesh. Because of what they had done once the selectors hung on in the hope that they might produce it again which gave the younger players few opportunities and when they did have a chance these same players were unable to take the pressure off as they once had done.

Fredericks the left handed opening batsman from Berbice, Guyana was the only new player who was able to establish himself in the side. He played in four Tests. He got into the side because Camacho, another Guyanese, lost form without ever getting much of a chance to regain it while Fredericks with his "eye" technique, did enough to retain his place. As the tour continued he developed a good deal and he looked a much better player in England the following May and June. None of the other new players, Davis, Edwards, Findlay and Camacho left much of a mark. Davis found himself batting at six or seven which never gave him the chance to play an innings. He played in the second Test mainly because of his medium pace seam bowling. It is unusual for a fast bowler to come into Test cricket at the age of twenty-eight and for a time it looked as if Edwards would emerge as one of the successors to Hall and Griffith. He was then very unlucky in his first Test Match at Melbourne and this made him lose heart. Even so he was a better bowler in Australia than Griffith and if he had been handled carefully he could have played a bigger part than he did. It was a surprising decision to drop him for the following tour of England. Findlay who comes from St. Vincent, a neighbouring island to St. Lucia in the Windwards, had his horizons considerably broadened, but with Hendricks wicket-keeping well he never had the chance of playing in a Test Match. He is a competent wicket-keeper however and is Hendricks' logical successor.

The chief West Indies success on this tour was Carew. Carew has been on the edge of Test cricket for a long time, but was too bottom handed and awkward to have made much of an impression. He was lucky to be picked for Australia, but having won a place again slightly against the odds, in the West Indies side for the First Test, he proceeded to look a very good player. He was standing straighter at the crease and his bottom hand was no longer so noticeable. He made runs at Brisbane and went on from there. Carew lets himself become very depressed by failure and his two innings at Brisbane gave him exactly the confidence he needed. While Carew was an unpredictable success, King from Jamaica was an all too predictable failure. He was not fast enough for the Australian wickets and was unable to make the ball move off the seam.

But all these West Indians never really lost their natural *joie de vivre* in spite of their misfortunes on the field. While wickets were falling in a Test Match there would be a continuous torrent of chatter and laughter from those in the pavilion. On aeroplanes, in buses, beside swimming pools, high pitched bursts of laughter would be forever punctuating English spoken at West Indian pace which is fast, and with the West Indian accents. Stores from previous tours, from last night, from yesterday's cricket with a lot of amusing mimicry thrown in. In all that they did in four and a half months in Australia, they were simply living a gay uncomplicated Caribbean existence in another part of the world.

A glimpse of the past

The Adelaide Oval is the most beautiful of the big grounds in Australia. Looking across from the main members stand the necessary amenities of a cricket ground blend satisfyingly with a rich panorama of green foliage coming from a myriad of different trees and shrubs starting just outside the ground and stretching back to the banks of the canal and beyond. The trees range from the various types of gum tree which are almost weeds in Australia, to palm trees and, half left by the scoreboard, to a Moreton Bay fig tree which at some time or another becomes the temporary resting place of every starling in Adelaide. Between them the trees and shrubs show off all the shades of green all jumbled up together so that one could almost be looking at a contemporary wallpaper design.

There are no stands on the far side of the ground, the outer as it is known in Australia, and this green is the backcloth to the cricket interrupted only by the tall Victor Richardson gates. The picture is helped too by the range of hills which stretch mistily across behind them on the other side of the city. They have lately become scarred by a vast and ever-growing quarry, but they still form an effective frame. Nearer to behind the huge scoreboard the spires of the Cathedral stick up out of the green and help to give the ground its serene, reflective atmosphere. The Adelaide Oval does not have the urgency of the Sydney Cricket Ground, nor the concrete vastness of the Melbourne Cricket Ground which seems to turn cricket into a gladiatorial combat, but an open friendliness of its own.

It was in this setting that the West Indies' flair for producing the unexpected and the dramatic flickered momentarily back to life in what was no more than a final death throe. At the end of five days cricket 1,764 runs had been scored and just 20 runs and one wicket separated the two sides. In a last hour of unbelievable excitement Australia threw away certain victory and with the help of three run outs in this time, the West Indies came desperately close to winning. It was the type of finish in which these West Indians had often been involved during the last decade and it produced all the tension and excitement which is unique to cricket and so memorable.

For more than four and a half days some splendid cricket was played, but without giving any hint at what was to come. Yet again the West Indies threw away the important advantage of winning the toss on a glorious batting wicket. Australia then built up a huge score and seemed to have effectively shut the West Indies out of the game. Coming into bat a second time 257 runs behind, instead of throwing their wickets away as they had done at Melbourne and Sydney with the circumspection of the Gadarene swine, the West Indies seemed collectively to sense the indignity of the situation and for the first time since the First Test they batted as if they were trying to prove themselves.

They all made runs and made them well, but they still were unable to rid themselves of the infuriating habit of throwing their wickets away when well set. Twenty-five minutes before tea on the fourth day they found themselves at 492 for eight which was 235 ahead with more than eight hours left. They had fought back bravely but defeat was still inevitable. Even now they had not been able to produce the concentration to defeat the untiring persistence of the Australian bowlers. It was then that Hendricks came out to join Holford. Neither of them had shown anything like their true ability with the bat through the tour, but for the next two hours and twenty minutes they both batted as well as they can ever have done and with the determination which at the last none of their betters could find. When Holford was out in the last over of the day they had added 122 for the ninth wicket and with one full day left the West Indies were 357 runs ahead and surely safe from defeat.

The Australians had lost the initiative for the first time since Brisbane and with Sobers and Gibbs to take advantage of any wear in the wicket on the last day, a West Indies victory was conceivable. Australia's final target was 360 in 344 minutes which on the fifth day of a Test Match looked impossible. But they were given a magnificent start by Stackpole and the ruthless determination of Lawry, Chappell and Walters took over as they set their sights on victory and continued to score quite safely at a remarkable rate and from first seeming an impossibility, an Australian victory became a possibility, a probability and then a certainty. Sobers had not got the bowling to check batsmen in this form. When the last hour began in which fifteen overs had to be bowled, Australia were 298 for 3 needing 62 more of 120 balls with Chappell and Walters batting well. Then after a tired stroke against Griffith had cost Chappell his wicket, three batsmen were run out in the space of seven runs and Sheahan and Connolly, Australia's last pair had to play out the last 26 balls of the match when Australia were left 20 runs short of victory.

The framework itself was dramatic, but it contained some glorious moments of cricket, which although a part of the whole, gave the game its own individual identity session by session and were in their way as memorable as the last hour. In their own distinctive ways the older West Indians all gave satisfying glimpses of their powers and in the second innings particularly there were moments when one might have been running through an old film.

Sobers of course is Sobers. A law unto himself with a cricket bat in his hands. He has no need to respect a bowler's reputation, it seems that all he has to do is to be in the mood. In the first innings he half-strode half-sauntered out to the wicket, the innings in ruins at 107 for 4, the top half of his body leaned forward in his own angular way. His shirt was still unbuttoned almost to the waist and his collar was turned up and the frown was on his forehead. As Sobers walks to the wicket anticipation grows with every step. At the wicket he batted like a cultured tidal wave. No matter where the Australians bowled he went for them instinctively using his height, his reach, his footwork and all the other gifts nature gave him in such quantity for playing cricket. He reached 50 in 44 minutes and 100 in 117 minutes and yet he never seemed to be in a hurry. It did not seem possible that a cricketer of this ability could be on the losing side. Sobers is a cricketer of the moment. This innings may retrospectively have seemed similar to ones at Georgetown or Kingston or wherever, but there is something so immediately exciting about his batting that when he is in the middle it is purely a reminder of the present.

On the other hand late on the fourth day Kanhai's wiry flamboyance had a less permanent look to it. Well though he had batted one could not escape from the feeling that this was a glimpse of something which had gone before. He swept at Gleeson and fell on his back, but it was a less ebullient shot than when he had played it in England in 1963. Then suddenly after tea his concentration broke and he lifted his head driving at Connolly and was bowled. He departed head down, handkerchief tied round his neck, sweat glistening on his forehead and as he passed through the gate maybe he was thinking about the two hundreds he hit for the West Indies in the Adelaide Test in 1960/61.

Carew who established himself for the first time, seems to leave his innate cheerfulness in his cricket bag when he goes out to bat. He is a rather bent figure in stance, his face rapt in concentration and in the second innings he set about Gleeson whose mysterious spin with his middle finger bent back against the palm of his hands had made the West Indian batsmen so neurotic. He hit him hard and he hit him straight and showed what, with a little more thought and application, might have been done three Test matches before. A chewer like all contemporary batsmen, Carew often gave the impression of a man who was used to failing at the top level and could not believe in his own success. But every so often old habits would return as they did with a quarter of an hour to go on the third evening when he hung his bat out at Connolly and first slip did the rest.

The first hour the next day belonged to Griffith the nightwatchman and he battled well holding his bat very straight and the scowl on his face was indicative of his thoughts when as he interpreted, Butcher ran him out. Butcher had become a batsman who gleans rather than scores runs. He hits the ball to the boundary, but seldom in a memorable fashion. He is rather cramped at the crease and is the least eye catching although one of the most effective of the West Indies batsmen.

For 45 minutes of his innings the spotlights were focused exclusively at the other end where Nurse played a great innings in miniature. One of the most cheerful, open and delightful of cricketers, Nurse had several times hinted at his ability, but so far on the tour he had been unable to find the fluency which is the hallmark of his play. He is a handsome, upright strokeplayer with a fine sense of timing and now capless and neat in appearance he went through his full repertoire of strokes. However correctly they are formed it is never quite true to describe a West Indian strokeplayer as classical. Somehow there is too much urgency or *joie de vivre* or maybe sense of fun which is injected into the stroke through their own bubbling enthusiasm. His back-foot drives through the covers off the fast bowlers were breathtaking strokes and even Sir Donald Bradman described this as the finest innings of the match. But then to prove that Nurse like the other West Indians was frustratingly mortal he hooked at a long-hop from Gleeson, missed and was lbw.

Another fifty by Sobers served to underline what this cricketer is capable of and also what the West Indies as a whole could still produce. Butcher emerged from his shadow at the other end to hit Connolly for fifteen in an over and to reach his hundred. Then, after batting more than three hours drove a gentle catch to cover and, a small man, departed chewing rhythmically and phlegmatically looking at the ground just in front of him. Lloyd with his glasses appearing to be perched precariously on his nose played some handsome drives, but after Sobers had gone the way of lost concentration he followed and it was left to Holford and Hendricks.

Holford has a very young face which makes him look almost out of place in a Test Match. He is a cricketer who desperately needs the confidence of his own success and at the start of this innings he was uncertain when to go forward and when to go back and uncertain when to say "yes" and when to say "no". But he and Hendricks suddenly seemed to gather strength from the hopelessness of the situation. In his attractive upright style Holford played some elegant strokes and showed that he was the only West Indian prepared to use his feet to attack the spinners. Hendricks at the other end batted with a lot of common sense within his limitations. When he got a ball to hit he hit it and when he had one to block, he blocked it and must have taken a lot of smug pleasure in frustrating the Australians like this. When Holford was out in the last over of the day he came boyishly in, shyly looking at his feet, having batted as well as he did at

Lord's in 1966. The whole innings had promised a lot which failed to materialise and was fulfilled right at the end in the most unlikely way.

The first day of the match belonged to Sobers. He came in when the West Indies were already doomed to a salvage operation with the Australian bowlers right on top and yet for two hours he gave a perfect exhibition of controlled strokeplay. Time and again as he unwound stroke after stroke, the elegance, the grace and freedom and the natural movement of which Nureyev would have been proud, was there for all to see. It was batting at its very best and revealed the full genius of one of the greatest of all cricketers.

There was a good crowd to see and enjoy Australia's success. Packed tight together on the grass mounds at either end of the ground and in the stands and sitting and standing in the open on the far side. There were many brightly coloured parasols to protect them from the hot sun and vast quantities of beer were consumed and occasional pieces of advice like, "give it a go yer mug" reverberated round the ground, but they were seldom followed.

Australia pushed home her advantage on the second day and all her main batsmen played a part in their own distinctive ways. For the Third Test Match Lawry had put Stackpole up the order to open and had dropped Radpath down to four and this had paid off well. Stackpole is a sort of Milburn but three sizes smaller and he loves to hit the ball, believing a long-hop to be a long-hop no matter when it is bowled at him. Equally Redpath when freed from the cares of opening felt himself freer to play his strokes and looked a much happier player.

Overnight Australia were 37 for no wicket and 30 of these had been scored by Stackpole. He set off at a tremendous rate against Sobers and Griffith playing an attacking shot at almost every ball, but not indiscriminately, and continued the next morning. Stackpole is a cheerful man with a smile always around his lips and he plays cricket in the same happy way. Like all the Australians he is a very determined cricketer, but he is a delightfully gentle person.

The result of his onslaught here—he is as good a hooker as any batsman playing today—was to throw the West Indies back from the start bringing all the initiative over to Australia. When he was caught behind pushing forward to a leg break he had scored 62 out of 89 in 100 minutes and given Australia exactly the start they wanted. Meanwhile Lawry had been batting like Lawry. With almost no backlift he had been pushing and steering the ball for ones and twos and pulling anything short. Lawry's purpose in the middle is to bat Australia into the strongest position possible and he was doing just that. He gets most of his power from his forearms so that it gives all his shots a curiously foreshortened effect.

As a man and an opening batsman Lawry is something of a paradox. He has a good sense of humour with an unforgettable laugh and is always leg pulling. There is nothing humorous about the way in which he bats, but he is amazingly consistent and even if he does not laugh out loud when at the crease, his success and the frustrations he causes his opponents must make him smile inwardly. As a captain Lawry likes to win and he rightly does everything he can to achieve this. At home he has a large number of very successful racing pigeons which is another interesting side of a fascinating man.

Ian Chappell who had been the success of the tour played another fine innings. Chappell's success was based first on his footwork which is amazingly fast and sure leaving him perfectly placed to play every shot and then on the fact that he has learned to play equally well off both feet. Technically he is a fine player, but he is not an aesthetically satisfying batsman. There is a certain ruggedness about all his strokes and when he hits the ball he is obviously putting everything he had got into the stroke. His batting is in keeping with his character for he is in many ways a rugged down to earth straightforwardl person; strongly built and with a thick crop of hair. He also has a good sense of humour but there are no affectations about him. He has a good cricket brain and during the tour he succeeded Jarman as vice-captain.

He batted for 45 minutes with Redpath, after Lawry had pulled a long-hop to deep mid-wicket, and together they produced as good a piece of cricket as any in the series. Redpath, tall and slim, plays his strokes with precision and elegance, but occasionally without full awareness of his responsibilities. It makes him an exciting batsman to watch, but also explains why he played as many as twenty-eight Test

Matches before scoring his first century. There is a romance about Redpath's batting which is totally lacking in Chappell's. He is a more "will o' the wisp" type of player than most of the others. He is another who is always smiling and often playing practical jokes or being the victim of someone else's and is always good value to be with.

He and Chappell put on 78 in those 53 minutes mostly against the spin of Gibbs and Sobers. Although there was nothing in the wicket for them they are as good a pair of spinners as there is. But Chappell and Redpath dealt with them simply by using their feet. They were down the wicket and driving to almost every ball bowled and whenever they dropped short in defence they went back on their stumps to cut or to pull. Soon Gibbs was bowling near medium pace, but still they came to him and on such a splendid wicket they did not have to be right at the pitch to drive. After half an hour neither bowler knew where to pitch the ball. In these days when spinners are so often played with exaggerated care from the crease, this stand made splendid watching.

Walters came in after Sobers had held a fine catch at backward short-leg off Gibbs to get rid of Chappell, and he continued to build on the improvement he had shown making a hundred in the Third Test at Sydney. Two years in the army did Walters' cricket a lot of harm for it stopped him continuing to develop at an important stage, and being pushed straight into Test cricket on his release, he was in the unenviable position of having to try and live up to a reputation which had been acquired two years before.

There was also an innings of mixed parts from Sheahan who had a bad tour. It is true that he continually came in when Australia were past 300 for 4 which did not give him the chance to build an innings, but he continually got himself out when well set. At his best Sheahan is the most attractive of the Australian batsmen. A tall man, he stands upright and plays his shots with great elegance. His off-drive is the nearest Australia can get to rivalling Graveney. On this tour Sheahan gave the impression that he is not as yet mentally tough enough for the needs of Test cricket. He also showed that when he is out of form he plays one of the worst looking sweep shots in the game.

The Australians were taken past 500 by a final flourish

from McKenzie who used power and reach to drive with tremendous force. When he pulled Gibbs for a big six it must have seemed the final straw to the West Indians who were looking thoroughly dejected and demoralised in the field with only Hendricks who kept well throughout the tour to inspire them. It made their subsequent recovery seem even odder.

The final day began with the news that the West Indies were going to bat on. This way Sobers would have the use of the heavy roller which he hoped might do something to break up the wicket. They went on for six minutes scoring two more runs which means that in all 16 minutes were used up. At the day's end those 16 minutes would have been valuable to the West Indies, but if Australia had themselves had another 16 minutes would they have rushed to their own destruction in the same way?

There was a dramatic start to the Australian innings. In the first over Stackpole hit two thumping fours through the offside, but then hooked at a short one which went with tremendous power straight at Butcher's chest by the square-leg umpire. Butcher whose fielding had become a liability to the West Indies barely got a hand to it. Fifteen came off this over and 46 came in the first half an hour off six overs. The only serene figure on the field was a seagull which stood imperiously at square-leg while Griffith bowled most of an over. During this opening stand the importance of cricket to the Australians was superbly illustrated when a bishop with a dark suit, black homburg hat and his purple silk walked in front of the members stand with a transistor pressed hard into his right ear.

Although Stackpole scored 50 of the opening stand of 86, Lawry soon caught his mood and produced a splendid square drive against Griffith. The innings had been going for an hour in which time 75 runs were scored before Gibbs bowled the first maiden over. But as soon as Stackpole had reached 50, his third successive Test innings, he was caught behind as he swept at Gibbs. There was an ominous sign for Australia in Gibb's fourth over when one ball turned and kept low, but luckily for them it proved a false alarm and hardly another ball behaved oddly all day.

At lunch the West Indies were 106 for one in even time and afterwards the West Indies came out with two substitutes, Camacho and Davis, as Hendricks and Butcher had pulled muscles and Nurse kept wicket, but although they were now more sprightly in the field, Australia continued their onslaught. Chappell might have been run out if Nurse had taken Camacho's throw cleanly when he was 24, but there were no other chances until Lawry when eleven short of his century pulled another long-hop straight to square leg. The score was then 185 for 2 and an Australian victory was looking distinctly possible as Redpath joined Chappell who then reached his 1,000 runs against the West Indians on the tour soon afterwards.

When Griffith started to bowl what turned out to be the last over before tea, Australia were 214 for 3. A single was scored and Griffith ran in to bowl the third ball to Chappell. He reached the crease but swivelled round halfway through his delivery stride to break the wicket and appeal against Redpath who was a foot out of his crease backing up. Umpire Rowan, having no alternative, immediately put up his finger and Redpath, rather dazed, walked back to the pavilion. When they saw what had happened most of the West Indians sat down on the ground and covered their faces with their hands. When the over which took nine minutes was finished the players came into tea and Sobers brushed past his own side and went straight into the Australian dressing room to apologise to Lawry.

It was an unfortunate gesture by Griffith which had no place in such a fine game of cricket or indeed in any game of cricket. Cricket has always been a game where the spirit is as important as the letter of the law and although the laws entitle Griffith to do this there is a time-honoured convention which says' that the bowler must first warn the batsman that he is backing up too soon. Some people defended Griffith's action but if this was to become an accepted practice, it would ruin the game. As it is, most batsmen start to back up as the arm goes over and not when the ball leaves the hand and a bowler so inclined could probably run out a significant number of batsmen. But cricket has always been a game where the bowler has concentrated on getting out the batsmen at the striker's end.

At the tea interval Australia were 217 for three needing 143 in 120 minutes. Thirty-three came in the first 30 minutes with Chappell batting magnificently and again using his feet continually to Gibbs. The 50 stand between him and Walters came in 44 minutes and when Griffith relieved Sobers 13 came off his first over. When the clock reached five o'clock the score stood at 298 for 3 with Australia wanting 62 from the fifteen overs which have to be bowled in the last hour. By then they seemed certain to win an incredible victory and the West Indies were again looking dispirited in the field. The 300 came up and then Chappell, four runs short of his hundred played half forward to Griffith in a rather tired-looking way and was lbw when the ball hit him half way up the front pad which made the score 304 for 4.

Walters with Sheahan as partner went on to reach his 50, his lowest Test score in six innings, but in the same over Sheahan played Griffith to Sobers at shortish mid-wicket. There followed a classic "yes, no, wait" situation and both batsmen ended up in mid-wicket and Sobers' gentle throw to Griffith easily beat Walters. 315 for 5.

Three more runs were scored and then off the second ball of the fifth over Sheahan turned Gibbs to Holford fielding just behind the square-leg umpire. Sheahan seemed to change his mind again and Freeman was late in starting and Holford's throw to Hendricks got there first. The new ball was now available, but Sobers kept on with spin. In Gibbs' next over Jarman swept him for four and as he passed Sheahan on his way back to his crease, he whispered, "mind the short singles." The next ball he cut ten or twelve yards to Sobers' left at short third-man, sent Sheahan back, but seeing Sheahan so far committed, set off. Four long strides took Sobers to the ball. He picked it up in his left hand and off balance in mid stride and running the wrong way he threw to the bowler's end. As Jarman said afterwards, "I was about three yards short when suddenly the stumps exploded." Another manifestation of Sobers' genius had left Australia at 322 for 7.

By now news had filtered through to the city workers that extraordinary things were happening at the Adelaide Oval and the outer was now full of suited office workers who came down from the centre of the city only about ten minutes walk away when they had finished work. McKenzie took Jarman's place and it seemed obvious that Lawry had told him to play for time, but when they had added eleven, McKenzie lost patience and swept at Gibbs—the fourth ball of the eleventh over—and Camacho stood for several agonising seconds under a skied catch with the sun in his eyes at square-leg. He held it and Australia were 333 for 8.

Sheahan who was now in a real state of nerves having had a hand in all three of the run outs, played out the rest of the over. The next, the fourth last, was started by Griffith to Gleeson. He went forward to the sixth ball, there was a noise and it flew through to Nurse behind the wicket and there was an appeal. Umpire Egar paused and then raised his finger high above his head in the way of Australian umpires. Egar then turned to the scorers and indicated that Gleeson was lbw and not caught at the wicket. Gleeson himself walked slowly back much mystified in complete silence.

There were 26 balls to be bowled as Connolly joined Sheahan. He played the last two of Griffith's over down in front of him surrounded by close fielders. Gibbs then bowled a maiden to Sheahan who reached forward and stunned each ball as it pitched. Then with two overs remaining Sobers himself took the new ball. Most people had forgotten about it in the excitement. Connolly took guard with the whole West Indies side crouching round the bat and Sobers ran in. The first ball swung a long way down the leg side, the second ball swung a long way down the leg side and so did the third and the fourth. Sobers could not control the new ball. If he could have bowled a straight one it might have been enough. After each ball Gibbs gesticulated frantically from short-leg. The fifth went down the leg side. The sixth Connolly squirted between the short-leg, the seventh he played down in front of him and the eighth he snicked for four.

Gibbs then bowled the last over to Sheahan who again stretched comfortably forward to each ball and then turned and walked off the field and as they came in the crowd which had swelled enormously in the last hour gave the West Indies tremendous applause. It had been a great game of cricket and left the players and the spectators with more buts and ifs and might-have-beens than most games. It was too the last triumph of this old West Indian side and for this it will probably be remembered longest, but it was an even bigger triumph for the game of cricket.

For the future

When late in April the West Indies touring party walked for the first time through the Long Room at Lord's on their way to practice, the sounds of their studs muffled in the soft floor, another tour had begun. Less than a month after leaving New Zealand they found themselves on the other side of the world for another series against England. It was not three months since Sheahan had pushed back that last maiden over to Gibbs and only a year and a fortnight since Jones had played another maiden over to Gibbs at Georgetown to save the series for England.

Time had moved too relentlessly for some. Hall and Griffith did not get out of the aeroplane at Heathrow, nor did Nurse or Kanhai who had had a cartilage removed. In their places some eager unknown faces excited at the prospect of their first tour came down the stairway. These newcomers were conscious of the glories of the recent West Indies side mostly from what they had read, but they were not here to try and recapture anything, they were here with their own ways to make and it was up to them.

What began among the palm trees, the rum and the Mighty Sparrow fifteen months before and then moved on to the eucalyptus trees and the ice-cold beer of the Antipodes was continuing among oak trees, a good deal of rain and an army of MCC ties. It was a constantly changing panorama in which the game of cricket was the common denominator.

In this time West Indies cricket had moved through a semi-circle. A great side which had held on too long, had been badly beaten and now they had begun to build again for the future. This short tour was going to reveal something of the immediate future of West Indies cricket. By a curious set of coincidences within just a few months, a heart attack, a car crash and a snapped Achilles tendon had robbed England of her main batting strength and so for her too this was a summer for experiment with the anticipation and the apprehension this held. Fifteen months before it was unthinkable these two sides could in such a short time acquire so many new faces. While Sobers with all his unpredictable genius was still leading the West Indies, England had fallen back on Illingworth to do the job for them while Cowdrey's heel spent most of the summer encased in plaster.

In the West Indies cricket is a game of instinct and all the joy that this brings, while in Australia it is one of hard efficiency where victory and satisfaction of success count for a lot. In England, the home of cricket, the game is naturally deeply rooted in tradition, but for the moment it has become a tradition in a vacuum. English professional cricket is also an extremely efficient game, but with a distorted set of priorities. What it has in efficiency it lacks in imagination and too often this efficiency is used for the negative pursuit of safety-first tactics. The approach of both the players and the public to cricket in England has changed since the war. The amateur has gone from the game and as is inevitable and right in the modern world with county cricket being played in one form or another seven days a week, professionalism has taken over. The margin for error in English cricket has widened considerably, but at the same time the game has become more stereotyped and predictable and the players with the imagination to change this are becoming fewer and fewer.

Sobers and Illingworth typified the approaches of the two countries. Illingworth is a highly capable cricketer with a deep knowledge of the game, but with an utterly predictable tactical approach. He plays the game unsmilingly, determined like all true Yorkshiremen to win, but when he regards this as impossible he turns all his energies towards avoiding defeat. The sudden gamble or piece of inspiration which might turn imminent defeat into victory does not, because of its illogicality, come into his reckoning. As a captain and a player too, Illingworth does not have the instinct to produce the unexpected and this means that his side will seldom play imaginative cricket.

England won the series, 2—0, by playing efficient methodical cricket which was good enough for the job in hand although the West Indies' flair for the game almost brought them victory in the Third Test at Leeds, but the cricket that England played did nothing to help the game.

The side was a machine of eleven parts, each man there for a purpose which he fulfilled in the safest possible way. Sharpe, the only Englishman to take a game by the scruff of the neck when he made 86 in 100 minutes in the second innings, and Hampshire who scored a hundred in his first Test innings were exceptions to this in the Second Test at Lord's and Knott was always an exception, while Boycott's efficiency typified a Yorkshireman's approach to cricket. It was a tragedy that Graveney forced the disciplinary committee to suspend him by playing in a benefit match on the Sunday of the First Test for his delicate touches were badly needed. It was sad, but typical that after being set to get 332 in five hours at Lord's England should have settled for safety so early. Sharpe's magnificent innings showed what could so easily have been done with a different approach.

There is a dull conformity about much of life in England which can be seen twice a day in the faces and actions of the crowds in all the city and suburban railway stations in the country, as well as on the cricket fields. So many people unambitiously follow the inevitable pattern of modern life and settle for pushing the ball gently to extra-cover and running a single rather than for picking the bat up high and driving it over the fielders for greater rewards.

At this stage of the book Sobers needs no describing or explaining, if an explanation is possible, either as a player or as a captain. As a player on this tour he showed only too clearly the effects of far too much cricket over the preceding eighteen months. Since Christmas 1967 he had not had more than the odd week or two away from the game. He had played in sixteen Test Matches and two overseas tours as well as a full season for Nottinghamshire and this was too much for any player.

In England Sobers captained his side with more enthusiasm than in Australia and he appeared to have a tighter control of the sequence of events. This could have been the result of some pressure from behind or it may have been that with several new players in the party he felt that he could get the response from them that he wanted. In the final analysis it was remarkable that it was his own form with the bat that prevented the West Indies from drawing the series. On this tour he as well as the other experienced players were unable in the moments of high pressure to produce the necessary application and Sobers continued to show his lingering reluctance to bat higher than six. At times during the three months the West Indians produced some memorable individual pieces of cricket, but they could not find the consistency which is so vital to success.

Sobers' 74 against MCC at Lord's, Fredericks' two 60's and Lloyd's 70 in the Second Test, Shillingford's six wickets at Worcester at the start of the tour, Butcher and Lloyd's stand at Swansea, their final exciting victory at Southampton when Fredericks, Lloyd and Sobers enabled them to score more than 350 in the last innings of the match and Sobers' remarkable bowling in the second innings of the last Test. From time to time these exciting cricketers revealed the full range of their instinct and this short tour of England showed that there is a rising generation of West Indian cricketers who will take on as the older players drop out, and without letting their country down either. Davis, Foster, Fredericks, Camacho, Findlay, Holder and Shillingford should form the basis of the West Indies side for the next few years, but their biggest problem, finding a successor for Sobers, still awaits an answer and short of playing fifteen in their side it will simply be unanswerable when it comes.

The change of environment when playing overseas faces the West Indians with as big a problem as any other touring side. The first overseas tour for a West Indian could be a bewildering experience. It is strange for a man who has lived in, say, the poorer part of Kingston suddenly to find himself living in luxurious hotels in England. The formality of England takes some getting used to. The weather and the cold have to be accepted, the slower and more deliberate pattern of life has to be understood and driving into London for the first time after coming, like Shillingford, from Dominica in the Windward Islands, presents many staggering contrasts. The first game of the tour was at Arundel Castle against the Duke of Norfolk's XI which was many worlds away from the last game they had played in the West Indies.

The West Indians themselves however do not change. Whether it is Australia or England they are able to go on being themselves. Their enthusiasm for living, their sense of fun and their excitable natures shine through everything.

When playing cricket in England, the West Indians attract their fellow countrymen to the cricket grounds and they are supported noisily and demonstratively just as they are at home, but this in itself does not affect their cricket. They bat, bowl and field in the way in which they are accustomed whether it is in Australia where because of the immigration laws there are none of their fellow countrymen to give them support, or whether it is in England where those that are there do their best to recreate a Caribbean atmosphere, but against the Anglo-Saxon backcloth look absurdly out of place. A West Indian in a green tail coat dancing and shouting in the free seats at Lord's is going to cause a lot of amusement and the dancing and shouting that goes on round the boundary when a four is hit, colours the scene, but without being the real thing. Mount Gay rum does not, after flying for nine hours between Barbados and London, taste quite the same. In the West Indies the Test players found the constant interruptions caused by high spirited spectators invading the field as irritating as their opponents. The West Indians do not gain stimulus from their fellow countrymen as spectators, rather they are both as involved as each other, one with the bat, the other with reaction.

An Englishman's involvement with cricket is as undramatic as most of the English crowds, but it is no less intense because of this. But the Englishman now lives in an age when the Breathalyser Test has forced him to desert the old and uniquely picturesque country pubs in small villages or out on their own in the country which used to act as a magnet to the neighbourhood. He has to settle for his less attractive "local" because it is within walking distance, or maybe he goes to the off licence and drinks at home. Drivers lose their licenses after three convictions for speeding and so everyone travels at the same speed. But in spite of this England is a country of great physical beauty and its people have great character, but at the moment the emphasis is too much on the urge to conform. The country is accordingly producing cricketers who know all about defensive pad play. If the mood of a country is faithfully reflected in its cricketers, England may have to wait awhile before a sense of adventure based on imagination comes back to its cricket.

But who knows? Australia and Chappell and Lawry and

company have been thrown off course by the South Africans while the gay but so different West Indian islands and countries are throwing up another generation of cricketers. They come from the same diverse backgrounds as their predecessors and have the same live West Indian instincts which enable them to play the game in the same way. Whether they develop the ability to match up to their recent side remains to be seen, but cricket will continue to unwind and develop in step with its environment as it has done during these eighteen months. Not all West Indian cricketers will bat like Sobers and Kanhai and they will not all bowl like Hall and Griffith, not all Australians will have the ruthless determination of Lawry and a generation of imaginative English cricketers will appear again one day.

Afterword

My first book was inspired more than anything by my enjoyment of touring. I had acquired a taste for it when I went to India to cover Mike Smith's England side in 1963/64. The tour to the West Indies four years later when Colin Cowdrey's side beat that great West Indian team captained by Garry Sobers, which was getting just a trifle long in the tooth, was an unforgettable experience. It remains as perhaps the most exciting series of Test Matches I have ever covered. Four of the five matches went down to the wire.

England should have won the first two; the second in Jamaica precipitating a dramatic riot which needed teargas to end it. They won the Fourth after Sobers had made an extraordinarily generous declaration and drew the Fifth over six days with the last pair of Alan Knott and Jeff Jones managing to see out the last few overs.

The cricket was exciting and so too were those lovely West Indian islands. Jamaica, with the rough and ready Kingston and Spanish Town contrasting so acutely with the upmarket tourist havens of Montego Bay, Ocho Rios and the rest on the north coast. There was the tranquillity of Barbados with contrasting Caribbean and Atlantic coasts and the thrills and spills of Harry's Nitery in downtown Bridgetown; and Trinidad consumed in the New Year by the annual pre-Lent celebration of Carnival where the whole island goes on a lengthy bender. Finally we came to the South American mainland and Guyana with the Dutch colonial city of Georgetown, the huge Demerara and Essequibo Rivers, the communist government of Forbes Burnham, a trip down the Kimune tributary off the Demerara to Santa Mission which was real Amazon country. All this and so much more and for me these adventures were just as exciting and memorable as the cricket which reflected so well the life going on around it.

Toward the end of 1968 I made my first visit to Australia

where Sobers's West Indian side was doing battle on another five-match series. Having been a cricket nut since the age of seven when I first listened to the snap crackle and pop of the atmospherics during those thrilling early morning commentaries from Australia during the 1946/47 tour by England, Australia was the country I wanted to visit more than any other. From my first schooner of beer in the old mining town of Kalgoorlie where I watched the West Indies first game of the tour, to the Gabba in Brisbane, it was in its way, as exciting an experience as the West Indies had been at the start of the year. Sobers himself and Lance Gibbs spun The West Indies to victory in the First Test. Thereafter their bowlers were flayed unmercifully by the bats of Bill Lawry, Ian Chappell and Doug Walters, and Australia won the series with ease. The Harbour, the Opera House, Peter Doyle's eponymous seafood restaurant in Watson's Bay were as gripping for me as events at the Sydney Cricket Ground. In Melbourne, Toorak and South Yarra, the Real Tennis court in Richmond, the Lawn Tennis at Kooyong, Christmas at Portsea and the Yarra Valley wines played their part as much as the huge stadium that was and still is the Melbourne Cricket Ground, the home of the 1956 Olympic Games. My memories of Perth, Adelaide and Tasmania are all as delightfully intermingled.

When I returned to England in February 1969 it had plenty to live up to. The common denominator with that summer's cricket in England was a three-Test series, also against the West Indies. These battles were played out to the backdrop of England's dark, satanic mills which seemed to me to be every bit as much depicted in the cricket as the characteristics of the West Indies, and then

Australia had been, in the game as it had been played in both those two countries. It was these thoughts that merged into my first, perhaps rather naive, plunge into a literary adventure.

About the Author

CRICKET HAS BEEN at the centre of Henry Blofeld's life since he first leaned to play the game at the age of seven. His first cricketing mentor was Miss Paterson whose splendid swingers went both ways when she bowled to him at Sunningdale School. He somehow managed to pass an exam to get to Eton where he played cricket against Harrow at Lord's when he was fifteen. Until he was seventeen he played with some success as a wicket keeper and an opening batsmen, and was in the Eton eleven for three years from 1955 to 1957, the last year as captain. In 1956, at the age of sixteen, he score a hundred for the Public Schools against the Combined Services in their annual two-day game at Lord's, joining Peter May and Colin Cowdrey as the only other two schoolboy players to have done so.

Then in June the following year came a severe road accident when he gallantly took on a bus with his bicycle and took no further interest in this world for 28 days. He made a remarkable recovery, but never played cricket with such promise again. He went to King's College, Cambridge where he never scored a run against the examiners and was kicked out after two years. He somehow blagged his way into the Cambridge side in 1959 and had the luck to play in first-class matches against Denis Compton and the great Australian all-rounder, Keith Miller, making a first-class hundred against MCC at Lord's.

After a two-and-a-half year spell in the City of London, bowler hat and all, he decided to see if he could write about cricket. However, the first article he ever wrote was about a second eleven football match in 1956 for the *Eton College Chronicle*. It earned him a robust interview with the headmaster for being rude about Bradfield School which was not a particularly auspicious omen for a career in journalism.

The Times decided to use Blowers, as he is affectionately know, as a freelance cricket writer in 1962. The following year *The Guardian* decided that they would find a home for his cliches and he remained with them as a freelance until *The Independent* set up shop at the start of the eighties. By then the *Sunday Express* also provided a home. He also wrote for the *Observer* and the *Daily Telegraph*.

In 1975 he joined BBC's panel of cricket commentators when he joined the famous *Test Match Special* team for two one-day games against Australia. His years were spent watching county and a certain amount of Test cricket in England - there was only one year when he commentated on every Test for TMS - and in the winter he toured the cricket playing world. He probably watched more neutral series overseas than those involving England and he often worked for more than one newspaper and often the BBC as well.

For about fifteen years he spent part of each winter in Australia where he wrote a column for *The Australian*. He also worked for a network of commercial radio stations led by Radio 2UE in Sydney who broadcast an alternative form of commentary for the international games, to the rather more staid government owned ABC. Blowers spent a month or two most years thereabouts in New Zealand where he became a member of the TVNZ commentary team.

Blowers began to write books in 1970. He has written in excess of fifteen titles, mostly about cricket, as well as two autobiographies, *A Thirst for Life* and *Squeezing the Orange*.

His theatrical career began in 2002 when Dudley Russell, a theatre agent and husband of poet Pam Ayres, thought he would be able to do a one-man show. Although cricket inevitably forms a part of these shows, they are really more about the extraordinary life he has led and the fascinating people he has bumped into along the way.

His family name was of course pinched by Ian Fleming for the name of one of his chief villains, Ernst Stavros Blofeld, in the *James Bond* books. He met Fleming who introduced him to Noël Coward at a lunch party in Jamaica. Coward became a friend and Blowers tells some highly amusing stories about him. Clive Dunn, also known as Corporal Jones from the BBC TV series *Dad's Army* was also a friend and another source of some splendid stories.

Blowers also does his share of after dinner speeches, and his distinctive voice has been used for a number of radio and television commercials, and he has also appeared on several TV shows such as the BBC's *Room 101* and ITV's *Celebrity Chase Special*. He also does work for his great friend, David Folb who founded The Lashings World XI, which fields an eleven of international cricketers. They play thirty odd matches a year in England taking famous cricketing names to parts of the country which would never expect to see them. This does a lot to spread the gospel of cricket and is a great boost for the game in the UK. Lashings go on a short tour each spring to Abu Dhabi where they stay at the Famous Emirates Palace Hotel and play some games on that hotel's beautiful ground.

His cricketing days are fewer now and and he commentates for *Test Match Special* on about twenty-five days Test and International cricket in England each summer and continues to write a few cricket columns a year for the *Daily Express*.

He mainly concentrates these days on his one-man show which has reverberated around Britain's provincial theatres for over a decade. More recently he has also done two-man shows with former *Test Match Special* producer Peter Baxter.

Blowers has also teamed up with John Bly, the furniture expert from *The Antiques Roadshow* who knows more about Chippendale than Chippendale did himself! They performed a two-act show at the 2010 Edinburgh Festival - a chat sitting round the fire with a bottle or two within easy reach, talking about the more ghastly aspects of modern life: political correctness and 'elf 'n safety and the lack of characters in today's world!

Everywhere he has gone, on countless cricket tours around the world, Blowers has lived life to the full regarding each day as an orange and squeezing it dry of the last drop of juice before moving onto the next day.

He is a medical freak having defied a heart by-pass operation which went horribly wrong, a gall bladder that behaved like a deprived monster, picking up the dreaded MRSA along the way. Since then, back and hip operations have followed two-a-penny, but all have been submerged by guffaws of laughter and bottles of Burgundy (both red and white) and life still goes on in capital letters.

Blowers has led a varied, entertaining and extremely full life, has always been, and continues to be outrageous and irresistible fun!

Also available by the Author

The Man Who Coloured Cricket

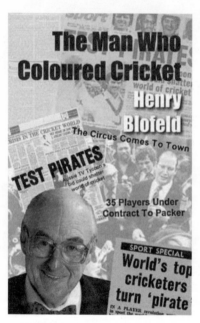

When Kerry Packer appeared on the cricket scene in the late seventies he revolutionised the game. Today's followers are used to coloured clothing and all the other razzmatazz that is now a part of cricket. But back in 1977 Packer's intervention was divisive and nearly broke the game completely. Players were ostracised by their nations and for a while it looked as if cricket might not survive.

Son of the newspaper tycoon Sir Frank Packer, the wealthy businessman shook the cricket world to the core. Henry Blofeld observed the goings on from his position as both a commentator and writer. In 1978 he compiled a detailed account of the events that unfolded, aided by his interviews with Packer, as well as the deposed English captain Tony Grieg.

He witnessed at first hand the Packer Tests in Australia; The Australia-India Test series; MCC play Pakistan and New Zealand; and finally the young Australian side that took on the 'Packer-filled' West Indies. In a mere seven-week period he witnessed all the then six Test-playing nations playing Test cricket. The first time that had been possible.

The Man Who Coloured Cricket is Henry Blofeld's detailed account of the developments that occurred throughout 1977-78. It also shows concern for the human dimensions of the controversy. The varied reaction of the English county players; overseas players; the legal tussles; the complex and surprising character of Packer himself; and the establishment figures with whom he did battle, are strands of the story expertly woven together to make a dramatic and moving story.

Complete with a new afterword in which Henry reappraises his thoughts, The Man Who Coloured Cricket is a truly enthralling read for new and old cricket enthusiasts alike.

The Man Who Coloured Cricket,
Wymer Publishing, 272pp. ISBN: 978-1-908724-35-9

Available from all good retailers. Quote the ISBN if needed.